TAKE THAT LEAP

Risking It All For What ***REALLY*** Matters

NIGEL J. BENNETT

978-1-7751533-0-6

Memory is a funny thing. Different people remember events and conversations differently. This book contains my best re-creation of the events and conversations in my life. For those of you who were there with me, please excuse me for any gaps in my memory or differences in our interpretation of how things happened.

Credits:

Cover photo by Ken Legg
Cover and interior design by Laurie Varga
Author headshot by Bob McKeachie

All other photos used throughout the interior of this book are the property of their owners and have been used with kind permission.

"*Awakening brings its own assignments, unique to each of us, chosen by each of us. Whatever you may think about yourself, and however long you may have thought it, you are not just you. You are a seed, a silent promise. You are the conspiracy.*"

Marilyn Ferguson, *The Aquarian Conspiracy* (1980)

Dedicated with love to my wife and lifelong partner Rieko,
our children Dylan, Devon and Kina,
everyone who has been and is part of our extended family,
all those who have awoken and
all who are still dreaming.

Together we are a conduit for change!

CONTENTS

PROLOGUE

"You need to write a book...!"

I can't tell you how many times I've had people say this to me over the years. Being gifted with dyslexia and Attention Deficit Disorder (what the doctors today call "inattentive ADHD"), I would just laugh and shrug it off.

They say travel enlightens. During a year-long walkabout of this amazing blue planet with my family in 2015, my response changed. Something someone said somewhere along the way enlightened me. I finally could see why so many people kept suggesting I write down my story and my ideas.

My life hasn't just been filled with adrenaline. I've been thrown into the business of environmental cleanup on an international scale. I've seen how the future of our entire fragile world and its inhabitants is being put at risk. I've struggled with trying to raise a family while building a business from the ground up. I've sought adrenaline rushes in the outdoors to balance the daily stresses of running a company. I've benefitted from the help and wisdom of countless people along the way. And I've been blessed with the opportunity to use my business as a platform to do good.

But that wasn't what really got me to start writing.

Our journey around the world made me even more aware than I already was of what I'll be leaving to my daughter, my sons and to young people everywhere. Our world looks pretty fucked up. It's going to take all of us—my generation and younger generations—working together to figure this out. And business is, so far, still the best framework we have for doing that. Fortunately, the old entrepreneurial myth—that the point of going into business is to grow it so you can sell it for a bag of cash—is going extinct.

I realized that I had a choice. I could sit back, stay where I'm comfortable with things I already know. After all, what can one guy writing a book actually do to help change the world? But then I realized, it's not just the exercise of writing a book that I would be undertaking. I would be taking another leap to bring this book and its message to you.

At that point, I decided to go for it.

In a way, I'm glad I didn't start out on this new-to-me adventure until then. When you're bringing up a family and running a business, you're constantly on the go. You don't have time or space to think about what you're learning, never mind writing. It wasn't until one day, deep in the Malaysian rainforest, that I realized I had finally reached a point where I had the time and space in my life to do just that. So I've used my freedom during the last couple of years to sort through all my adventures and select the ones worth sharing.

Personally, I'm not into reading blow-by-blow descriptions of someone else's life. They just don't engage me. So I looked at mine in terms of phases and themes. What you're about to read is organized into 14 chapters that follow those threads. The storyline moves back and forth through time and space, but, hey, what else would you expect from someone with the attention span of a squirrel?

One of the most important choices we ever will make is what we are going to do with our life. I hope that, through this book, I can inspire even just a few of you to become entrepreneurs, use your businesses to do good in the world, and create amazing and meaningful experiences for yourself and your family.

Then I will know I have used my freedom well.

CHAPTER 1
The Deep End

My heart was racing with adrenaline and fear. This long night drive from Alexandria to Cairo was terrifying. The headlights from oncoming cars and trucks blinded us as we sped along the desert road at 75 miles an hour, not slowing down as we weaved past goats, camels and broken-down trucks in the middle of the road. Occasionally flames lit up the roadside. It was only as we got closer, we would see the blackened flames came from tires that had been removed from trucks and set on fire to act as some sort of absurd hazard warning. Every time we passed one of these signal flares, the pungent smell of burning rubber hit my nostrils and black, sooty smoke filled my eyes. I knew from experience that some of these breakdowns were fake, set-ups to hook a good Samaritan into stopping to offer assistance. Then a band of thugs would rise from the darkness and rob you, kill you and leave your body by the side of the road without hesitation. Each time we neared a burning tire, George actually sped up.

Three-and-a-half hours later, I started breathing again at the sight of Cairo's lights slowly appearing in the distance. Whenever I entered the city in daylight, the great pyramids of Giza would be the first thing I saw in the distance through the thick smog. In the darkness, I was focused on what was right in front of me and I found myself thinking, once again, that the people here had been much better off 3,000 years ago. This place was actually devolving. At least, that is how my 23-year-old self was experiencing Egypt on this autumn night in 1988.

After entering the main city, we worked our way through small side streets filled with flimsy tents under which vendors sold everything from live chickens and Egyptian flatbread to nuts and dates from the Nile Delta. The scents of sweet spices and sandalwood perfume filled the air, until we rounded the next corner and my stomach turned at the odor wafting from open sewers. Small streets gave way to larger thoroughfares that we had to enter through chaotic roundabouts that beaten up cars and taxis were flying into with grand abandon, their drivers not paying any attention to lines on the road or who entered first.

We finally arrived at our destination at about 11 p.m. As soon as we stopped moving, I pulled on the door latch and jumped out of the car. I was happy to get out of the old black-and-orange rust bucket of a Fiat that had been my makeshift taxi for the past several months. Grabbing my bag, I ran up the steps of the hotel. Someone appeared from out of the darkness, quietly coming up beside me and grabbing my arm. "Follow my instructions. Don't say anything, look straight ahead and come with me quick." The urgency and anxiety in his voice were palpable. The man ushered me directly into the hotel and up the stairs to the second floor, where he led me down the hall to a door. Stopping briefly, he fumbled nervously for the key, then jammed it into the doorknob and forced the door open. He pushed me through the doorway inside the darkened room, saying, "Sit on the floor and don't speak." He closed the door and came to sit down beside me.

As we sat there side by side with the lights off, he whispered in my ear. "Your father is missing. I think he is in some kind of trouble. We checked in together but now he is nowhere to be seen." I turned to look at him, but could barely see his face. Every time I went to ask a question, he put his finger to his lips and gestured, "Shh, they are probably listening...". We sat on the floor together, staring into the dark, for what seemed like hours. I was deliriously tired and started nodding off....

Suddenly the phone on the old wooden desk across the room broke the silence with a guttural ring. Then a second time, "Brrrrrrring!" We both jumped at the sound. He sprang up and ran to the desk to answer the call. All I could hear him saying was "Yup, yup, OK, OK...." Then he looked through the darkness at me and said in a low voice, "It's for you."

I remember the day it all began. It was June 30th 1980, the day after my high school graduation. I woke to find an airline ticket on my pillow. The ticket was for a flight the very next day to Caracas, Venezuela. I had no idea then that I would be spending extended periods of time over the next decade in Venezuela, Brazil, Egypt, Malaysia, Thailand, Indonesia and China. And I definitely didn't think I'd be making my way in life by hanging out of helicopters and small fixed-wing aircraft as I photographed sensitive coastal areas for Bennett Environmental Consultants (BEC), my father's company.

Summer that year in Venezuela was hotter and more humid than usual. I wasn't used to the humidity, having just come from the colder climate of my hometown of Vancouver, Canada. The side door on the helicopter was stuck. I needed it open so I could sit on the side with my feet on the skegs to take the best possible photos of the lake. This trip was like many others I would make to help countries develop a national oil spill contingency plan. Computers were pretty much in their infancy at the time, so the work involved collecting data on the entire Venezuelan coastline from both air and ground and then plotting all this data on crude marine navigational maps using multiple translucent sheets of acetate overlaid on a map. Today we were flying out of the small town of Cabimas on the northeast side of Lake Maracaibo. Our flight path would take us in a clockwise fashion around the lake, first heading south to the bottom tip then up along the westernmost coastline, flying over Maracaibo, the largest city on the lake, and then up to the most northerly region, extremely close to the Colombian border, eventually finishing the circuit by returning to our starting point of Cabimas.

I turned and tried to slide the chopper door open with all my might. "Esperar a mi, amigo," said the friendly voice of a local oil company man sent along to assist me with these overflights. The door of the Bell helicopter was opened for me so I could begin shooting aerial photographs. The chopper flew south out of Cabimas towards Zulia province with me hanging out the door. Right away, directly below us, I could see the spaghetti of 25-year-old pipelines lying just beneath the shallow surface of the lake. Oil was seeping from many ruptures and breaks, presenting a problem much bigger than our client, the national oil company, realized. These corroding pipes, originally laid down by the British and Americans, had not been maintained properly since the government nationalized the industry in 1976. Spills had become more frequent, and our foreign expertise was desperately needed. In the thick, dense humidity, we could smell the stench of crude oil rising in the hot sun from off the water. I took photo after photo to document the environmental catastrophe.

We kept flying south to the foot of the lake. Here I took my first photos of indigenous peoples still living in shacks on stilts like they had for millennia, still hunting with blow darts for monkeys and other sources of food that lived high up in the canopy of trees in this rich green jungle. From this idyllic existence, we then turned north up the western side of the lake, flying over Congo Mirador on our way past Maracaibo.

My clothes were soaked with sweat from the heat and humidity. I was hanging out of the chopper with my headset half on, one side digging into my head, when I heard an agitated voice yell, "Alejamos de esta área o vamos a derribar!" Hastily translating with my basic understanding of Spanish, I thought the voice had said something like, "Move away from this area or we will shoot you down!" I felt a sense of panic rising inside me. I realized I was exposed and helpless in this position. There was nothing I could do but hang on tight.

Below in the green canopy, I saw several flashes of light. I didn't know if they were gun shots or the sun reflecting off something metal.

What the fuck! *I am about to die and I'm only 18 years old...*

The pilot began to argue with a man on the other end of the radio.

I had heard there was a large anti-Colombian government guerrilla presence known as FARC in the area below. This group of freedom fighters had been grabbing headlines around the world by blowing up pipelines, and the oil that flowed between Venezuela and Colombia was one of their prime targets. FARC's operations were funded by ransoms raised through kidnapping and acts of terrorism.

Our pilot suddenly pulled on his stick with a jolt, even though I was still hanging out of the chopper. One of our local aides yelled, "Cuidado, amigo!" ("Be careful, my friend.") He pulled me inside and added, "Esos tipos están **locos** ahí abajo!" ("Those guys are **crazy** down there!").

As the chopper veered away, I asked myself, *"What the heck am I doing here?"* I was thousands of miles away from home on my first work assignment after having just graduated from high school a month earlier. I could easily have been killed in an instant and no one back home would have ever known.

We all sat quietly, keeping words to a minimum for the next half an hour as we made our way back to the heliport in Cabimas. I was so eager to get out of the chopper that I jumped out even before the skegs hit the ground, keeping my head low as I ran away from the roar of rotating blades.

Soaked in sweat, I jumped in a cool shower as soon as I got back to my hotel room. I sat on my bed for seemingly hours with my head in my hands, trying to grasp the reality of what had just happened. A knock at my door and a familiar voice called me back to life. "Ey mon, wanna come wit me to a party tonight?" It was one of the many local workers from Trinidad, the only community I had in Venezuela at the time, who also spoke English. I looked up and thought, "You have no idea what I just went through." Staring at the door, I said, "Yeah".

Walking through the muddy streets of Cabimas together, we passed many huts with no doors. I could see people's eyes watching us from their hammocks. I was sure they were wondering as we passed by who we were. Eventually my friend stopped in front of one shack and said, "Here 'tis. You wanna some rum?"

I nodded and walked in, ducking my head as I passed under several hanging hammocks. In the middle of the mud floor, a group of Trinidadians were all chatting and having fun. In the corner, a close-and-play record player was blaring music that sounded roughly like steel drums. I was emotionally shattered from the day, still shaken by the close call with FARC and wildly pumped up on adrenaline. I thought good food and good company might take my mind off what had happened. The group shared some small dishes of pork and corn bread (arepas) and the rum kept flowing all night. We laughed together as I watched them dance for hours.

The next thing I recall I was vomiting in the sink of my room. I had no idea what time or what day it was. It was pitch black, so it probably was the middle of the night. The next time I came to, it was daylight outside. I felt even worse. The vomiting and diarrhea were uncontrollable.

I must have passed out again and again over the next few days. I tried to take a shower, but I lost consciousness. I don't recall how long I lay on the floor with the water of the shower running over me.

Suddenly I felt someone slapping my face. "Señor, señor!" I woke up to the startled voice of a young girl. I was sprawled across the bathroom floor, totally naked. The maid got me into bed and then left promptly. She returned later with a man, whom she said in Spanish was her uncle, a doctor. He looked after me for a few days. By this time, I had been out for at least a week.

I was still delirious and required hospitalization. Dave, one of our BEC crew from Canada, had just flown in and heard that I was really sick. He was able to get me together enough to fly to Caracas where he got me into a hospital. I barely remember what happened there. I was told that at one point I went a bit crazy and broke a chair against the wall. When I first came to, I found myself slumped on a gurney covered by a single filthy sheet. I glanced around the small dank room: the only feature was a broken sink surrounded by a puddle of rusty brown water. A doctor eventually arrived to diagnose me, telling me I had caught some type of parasitic infection. In the years ahead, the parasite would seemingly come alive again and again. But for the next few days, the doctors kept me hooked up to an IV, pumping me full of drugs and liquids to counteract the infection and my dehydration. When they released me several days later, I still felt terrible. The doctor who signed me out of the hospital gave me some antibiotics that he said would kill anything I had.

Fortunately, I had found a flat in Caracas a month earlier where I was able to stay. It had open cinder blocks for air circulation and a wooden door that I could close if it was windy or rainy. I was still pretty out of it and alone again, but at least I was in the city. Dave had flown back to Cabimas to continue our work there. My only job now was to fully recover.

The days and nights blended into one another. One night I was awakened by a raging storm. My cinder block wall had been open and my entire flat was soaked. Everything was dripping wet. I got up and tried to close the huge door across the front of the cinder blocks to stop the weather from getting in. It took all my strength to shut out that storm. I crawled back into bed, curled up in a ball in my wet sheets and actually started to pray to whatever god would listen. I remember saying, "If there is a god up there listening and if I live through this experience, I will thank you every day for the rest of my life." I prayed for quite some time before I fell asleep.

I spent the next decade from 1980 to 1990 jumping on airplanes to document how the pristine coastlines of the world were being impacted by oil spills. Most of the time, no one wanted us there documenting the total disregard for the environment and indigenous peoples that the oil industry continually displaced. All I saw, over and over again, were rigs with broken pipes leaking rivers of oil into oceans, rivers and lakes. Everywhere I went, witnessing the environmental degradation caused by the oil industry made me sick. On the one hand, I loved what I did: I loved seeing big blue and green water masses from the air and witnessing the extraordinary life beneath the waves. On the other hand, I was discovering that this environmental degradation and destruction was a global issue.

In 1988, I was back in Alexandria, Egypt. I had been working all over the country on and off for the previous five years. "Alex" had been our base. This morning, I was the last remaining staff member in Egypt, the rest of our crew having left the country a few days earlier. I was cleaning up the long-term apartment in which our team had lived in close quarters for so long. I was so glad to be wrapping up and finally going home to Canada. I had been really sick again over the past few days with diarrhea, a common complaint of international travelers in the 1980s. The night before, it had been so bad that I had actually been sitting on the toilet while vomiting into the bathtub. I had pounded back every medication I had, desperately trying to slow down this double ender. Not a good night.

"George", our friend and driver, was due to pick me up that evening and drive me to Cairo, where I would meet my father so we could fly to London together to attend a family wedding. At least, that was the plan.

As I packed up my belongings, I started to think about how hard it was going to be to say goodbye to George when we got to Cairo. We had hired him a few years before as a driver and he had done such a great job that we had kept him on for the term of our contract. He had become like family. A Christian living in a Muslim world, he was highly educated but, due to his beliefs, could only get a job as a taxi driver. For me, this was difficult to understand. I was worried for his well-being after we left the country.

George's taxi - Alexandria, Egypt (1988)

Later that afternoon, I took a break from packing up. I was feeling quite ill so I took one last walk along the broken sea wall of Alexandria out towards the Montazah area and the old palace gardens of King Farouk. Many of the apartment buildings here were falling down and leaning just like the tower of Pisa in Italy. The concrete in Egypt was of such poor quality that buildings would tilt and crumble, but people would still refuse to move out.

I had walked through the gardens many times before. This was my sanctuary away from the craziness of Alexandria. The sea lapped up against the retaining wall inside the palace grounds. I took a deep breath of sea air, looked out at the

Mediterranean and realized that this was it. I was finally leaving. My stomach reminded me that it wouldn't be a good idea to walk too much further this time. I turned around to head back to the apartment. As soon as I left the walled garden, several young boys wearing tattered clothes ran up to me with their hands out asking for money. Their eyes lacked hope. I gave them a few pounds as they said, "Shokran" ("Thank you"). I replied, "Afwan" ("You are welcome") and carried on back to our apartment to finish packing up.

As I walked up the steps to our building, I could hear something faintly in the background. It was a ringing sound. I realized it was our apartment phone, so I rushed to put my hand on the doorknob to our flat. I turned the key but the door was stuck, so I put my shoulder against the door and gave it a good push. It broke free and opened. I ran in and picked up the phone. "Hello, hello...?", I said. But the line was dead.

A minute later, it rang again. "Brrring, brrring!" I jumped and picked up the receiver. A voice I knew well said, "Have you heard from your father?" It was our CFO Clark calling from Cairo. "No," I said. "I thought he was with you?" He responded, "Yes, he was. We arrived together and checked into the hotel and agreed to meet in the bar for a drink. But he never showed up. I have no idea where he is now. Do you?"

> *What had happened? What was going on? Then again, we're talking about my father here. Maybe he just went for a walk or had to meet someone...?*

I told Clark to sit tight and I would be there in about three-and-a-half hours. By then, it was already getting late. The sun was down. That meant George and I would have to drive the dangerous desert road from Alexandria to Cairo in the dark. Not a good thing to have to do, even though I had driven this road many times over the past five years. But I knew even local Egyptians would never drive the Cairo-Alex-Mersa Matruh desert road at night: it was just too dangerous.

"It's for you."

It was 3:00 a.m. when I grabbed the phone receiver out of Clark's hand. All I heard on the other end was the very distressed voice of my father, who spoke in a confusing code. "Listen to me very carefully. This is the only call they will allow me from jail. Take the next bus and stay with Mike."

Then he hung up.

The phone went dead in my hand. I looked up again at Clark and whispered, "What the fuck is going on?"

> *We must all be in great danger or Dad wouldn't have spoken like that. I don't know what to do next....*

We sat on the cold floor of the hotel room in the dark for what seemed like hours, trying to make sense of what little my father had told us. He had said to Clark that he was being held by the police and that this was his one phone call. Finally I figured out his code: he must mean for me to take our original British Airways flight tomorrow to London and stay with my cousin Mike.

I didn't want to leave the country without my father. Clark argued with me. "You have to go. If they get both of you, they will have more bargaining power." I eventually agreed. I needed to take that flight in the morning.

After we slept on the floor for a few hours, I got up and splashed some cold water on my face. Clark took me out the back door of the hotel to where George was waiting to drive me directly to the airport. As we made our way through the city in the early morning mist, my mind was flying all over the place. I felt like I was in a tunnel and couldn't think straight.

> *What had happened to my father? Why was he in jail? What if my name has been passed to the police or the military?*

At the airport, I was nervous and agitated, certain that everyone was watching me. The woman at the check-in counter told me in her broken English that the British Airways flight to London was three hours late due to a mechanical problem but that I should check in now. The thought of sitting four hours in this dank airport—during which time the authorities could potentially find me—made me sick to my stomach. I nervously passed through several checkpoints, showing my passport each time. I was able to get through to my gate but had to wait ages for my boarding call.

When my flight was finally announced, a mass of people crowded the boarding area, pushing and jostling to the front. A bunch of military police appeared and started checking passports.

> *I am done for.... They know...they are looking for me.*

I slowly got up and joined the mob. Keeping my head down, I worked my way to the front where two guards stood with machine guns slung over their shoulders. One asked for my passport. I fumbled with the pages and then dropped it. I picked it up and passed it to him. He opened it to my photo page, lifted the passport up to my face and looked back and forth several times. He then passed the document back and said, "Pass." I walked down the gangway outside to a bus. As I passed through the door, the heat hit me like a brick. But the smell in the air was worse. It was the horrid smell again of sewage. My stomach retched and I gagged on my own vomit. I had to keep it together, so I swallowed. I could feel the burn as the vomit went down the back of my throat.

I boarded the bus, cramming myself in with the many Egyptians heading to London and the few foreigners. The bus lurched forward and drove toward a large DC 10, then stopped. Two more military troopers with machine guns stood at the bottom of the gangway to the British Airways plane, ready and waiting to check us yet again.

I tried to blend in with the Egyptians but I stood out like a sore thumb. I walked to the ramp with my passport open to my photo page this time. One of the troopers looked at it and said, "Bennett?" I still could taste the vomit in my mouth. Somehow I muttered, "Yes." He looked at me again for a moment. "Pass." I moved toward the stairway and tripped on the first step. Both guards looked around at me. I smiled my innocence in their direction and carried on up the stairs. As I entered the plane, the beaming BA stewardess asked to see my boarding pass. I showed it to her and she promptly said in a kind British Accent, "Welcome aboard British Airways."

I took my seat in the back of the plane in what was the smoking section at the time. People were lighting up cigarettes all around me. I started coughing so I reached up and turned on the air. I carefully sat back and took a deep breath of smoky air.

In a few minutes, the captain came on the intercom and announced, "We are fully loaded and ready to take off. Flight crew, please take your seats." We taxied out to the runway. I dared to look out the window as we began to speed faster and faster towards takeoff. Through the haze, the lights of Cairo faded into the distance.

I was finally headed for London.

CHAPTER 2
Minefields

Chicken or fish? Chicken or fish?

I could hear an echo in my head.

"Sir, would you like chicken or fish?"

I looked up out of my daze to see the stewardess smiling down at me, asking what I would like for lunch. I looked up and replied, "...ah, fish."

As I peeled back the hot tinfoil cover from my tray, two new questions kept repeating over and over in my head.

What is going to happen next? And what can I do?

That flight to London gave me a chance to reflect on the last few years and days and what might have landed my father in jail. I had seen my fair share of environmental degradation in the countries we'd worked in. Nobody seemed to be doing anything about it. Everything always seemed to be kept under wraps.

In lands where everything seemed to be falling apart and getting the basic necessities was a challenge, I had often felt helpless to make change. Oil companies were starting to remove their corporate logos from everything that the public could view, such as tank farms, oil terminals and trucks. If anything did happen, not having their name visible everywhere would slow down the imminent barrage of press and the public outcry that would be headed their way.

As we flew away from Cairo, I was reminded of a particular piece of survey work I had done in 1986 in the Gulf of Suez with LP, my business associate at the time, and the helicopter trips I'd taken out of Ras Gharib, Egypt's northern-most municipality on the Red Sea. My father had hired LP, top of his class, right out of British Columbia's Institute of Technology. A brilliant ideas guy when it came to all things technical, LP had previously worked with me in Brazil back in 1982 setting up a joint venture manufacturing facility in Sao Paulo, Brazil.

It was 5:00 a.m. in Cairo when three oil company men from the General Petroleum Company arrived in an old Ford Explorer to pick LP and I up at our hotel. We both jumped in the back bench seat and I said, "OK...we're ready to go." In the early morning light, the SUV headed east out of Cairo toward the Gulf of Suez. We drove for what seemed like forever through a dry, flat, barren landscape that looked more like the moon than the flowing sand dunes of the 1981 action-adventure film *Raiders of the Lost Ark.*

After two hours of semi-conscious bumping around in the back, LP and I were both feeling pretty rough. Eventually, I felt a slight breeze on my face. I gingerly opened one eye and thought I could see the green waters of the Red Sea in the distance. We turned to the right with a bump, veering off the main road onto a dusty gravel track that would take us south of the city of Suez. This was a small two-way road with huge potholes, half pavement, half sand, half gravel. We drove south for another hour until I called out, "We need to stop *now*!" LP, a normally robust-looking man whose short stature and dark hair revealed his Italian heritage, looked as if he was going to throw up any minute. He staggered off in the direction of the water, then bent over and vomited, trying not to let our oil company escort see. I chuckled, feeling pretty much as if I could do the same any second. I took a few photos of the landscape, giving LP time to get some air before we clambered back into the rust bucket.

The heat of the day began to rise. The only thing holding us together as we huddled on the bench seat in the back of the truck was that we could see the sea just beyond the broken rock of the desert. There was no beach, just garbage and a pungent smell of oil in the air. At times, the road brought us so close to the water that we could see the waves breaking. Somehow the water looked quite different from what we expected.

My eyes kept coming back to the single strand of barbed wire that stretched along the side of the road. Every so often, the wire would be interrupted by a piece of rusted metal with a skull and crossbones grossly painted across it.

These warning signs marked active minefields that had been laid during the Six-Day War between Egypt and Israel in 1967. The Egyptian Army and the oil companies were still in the process of jointly de-mining the coast, so they said, but with the shifting winds the mines would appear and, just as quickly, disappear. We could actually see where the wind had blown sand away to expose mines and they were just lying there on the other side of the single strand of barbed wire.

"Rumble...rumble...rumble.....ssssssss." Our truck shuddered and then stopped. The oil men started yelling in Arabic. They jumped out and opened the hood, only to have a cloud of steam burst up at them. They were all squabbling about something. LP, being a pretty good mechanic, took a look at the engine and saw there were multiple problems. We filled the leaking radiator from the only jug of drinking water we had and waited thirty long minutes to let the engine cool down.

When the truck started up again, we all crammed back in and carried on our way south. At Ras Gharib, there was a military truck with troops checking passports. The soldiers, unshaven and in dirty uniforms, wanted nothing to do with expats like us. They grudgingly looked over our documents and then opened the barricade to let us pass.

We pulled over at a rest stop just on the other side of the barricade to get more water. While the radiator was being refilled, LP and I slipped inside a concrete bunker looking for a cold drink. At the sight of a Coca-Cola® machine against the far wall, LP said, "Thank God!". We were so thirsty and dehydrated: he rushed over to it, opened the top and thrust his hand inside. In less than a second, he pulled his hand out. The machine was hotter inside than the air outside. It was empty, and probably had been for years.

A man in a long, thin robe approached us and said something in Arabic. The oil men interpreted for us. "He offers you tea." We accepted and soon were sitting on plastic chairs outside under a bit of shade created by a sheet of metal overhanging the bunker's roof. The temperature kept climbing. It must have been 104 degrees Fahrenheit by now. The man came back with several small glasses and a brass pot of hot tea. He wiped each glass off with his dirty sleeve and placed them all in the middle of the table. He then started pouring boiling hot tea into each murky glass. Within seconds, the glasses were buzzing with hundreds of flies, all attempting to land. Within a minute, we must have had twenty-five flies perched on each glass. LP looked at me and said, "Let's get the fuck out of here." Parched with thirst, we loaded up our empty bottles with whatever water the rest stop could spare, which was, of course, dirty and non-drinkable, and boarded the wreck of a vehicle.

We continued south for a few more hours, with the truck breaking down about every thirty minutes and our supply of radiator water dwindling with each stop. Finally, we arrived at an official "guest house" run by General Petroleum Corporation, the poorest of all the oil companies in the country and the only one that was 100% Egyptian. LP and I entered and asked if there were any beds. They pointed us to a room. Two single beds with mattresses that were probably two decades old greeted us. We both sat down, creating a cloud of dust in the room. We were so tired we didn't care. We lay down and crashed for a few hours, only to wake when the oil men called us for dinner. We were hungry—that is, until we saw the food.

We decided to skip dinner and take a walk to get some sea air. As we stepped out of the bunker of a guest house, the overwhelming smell of oil hit us. We walked along the coastline, a beach covered with garbage, old chicken pens, plastic and, worst of all, OIL. As far as the eye could see, a thick coating of tar covered the entire intertidal zone of the beach. Looking out at the surf, we realized that the waves frothed with oil.

What the hell have they done here?

The waves were *made* of oil! We looked at each other, almost gagging with the smell. LP said, "We are *not* staying here."

We rushed back to the bunker, only to find the oil men playing Egyptian Ratscrew, a card game favored by locals. We told them we had to leave, that we could no longer stay. The oil men were shocked. It was considered a privilege to get to stay in the guest house. LP told me to tell them that he refused to stay. So they packed up and we climbed back into the Explorer and headed south.

As night fell, the desert grew dark very quickly. We were told by the oil men that they were very nervous and that we should have remained at the guest house. They knew it was very dangerous to travel at night due to bandits. The truck kept overheating, but we pushed on. We needed to get to some-place safe.

I had remembered that I stayed at a Club Med a year earlier that was about another hour further south in Hurghuda, so we headed there. It was very late when we arrived and the place looked abandoned. The Club Med, previously run by the French, had been taken over by Egyptians who changed the name to MagaWish. There was no other place to go. We asked if we could stay the night and said we would pay. It was full, but they agreed that we could use a staff bungalow.

After a good shower, some real food and a night's rest, we both felt much better. Thanking our hosts, we carried on for our scheduled visit of a Shell oil compound just north of the area in Zeit Bay. Shell had a joint venture there called SUCO, which was owned by the Egyptian General Petroleum Company and Shell Oil. We were to advise on environmental planning issues that the new facility would need to implement once completed.

This was in the 1980s, when the Gulf of Suez was a hotbed of new exploration for Egypt and the international oil community. A national law at the time limited any foreign company wishing to explore and produce oil from the Gulf to a maximum 49% stake in any project: the Egyptian government would keep control with the remaining 51%. Many foreign companies including Shell, Amoco, ENI and BP had agreed to these terms and were heavily involved in the Gulf for the next thirty years.

After about two miles, we finally turned off the bumpy main road to head back towards the Gulf to meet up with "James", a SUCO employee and expat Scot, who had contacted us by radio with our rendezvous coordinates. James was sitting in the middle of the desert in his truck. He hailed us to follow him in our vehicle, guiding us to where SUCO was going to build the new marine oil loading facility, stopping often to point to specific areas to be developed. I was bursting to take a pee. When we finally did stop, I jumped out of the truck and wandered off through the dirty sand and over broken rock to relieve myself. As the pressure in my bladder subsided, I scanned the flat horizon and asked myself yet again, *"What the hell am I doing in this place?"*

Suddenly, a yell came from where we had left the trucks.

James was yelling at the top of his lungs. "Hey Nigel...**don't move**! You're in a minefield! Our guys have been working around the area here and took down the wire. There may still be some live mines around." My heart started pounding out of my chest. He hollered again.

James's voice hammered in my head, "Can you see your footprints? Turn around slowly and try to retrace your steps."

I gulped and looked down at the wet sand where I had just urinated and then looked slowly around at the broken rocks, sand and shale all around me. I could kind of see where I had stepped. Ever so carefully, I found a boot print. I stepped in it. I saw another and another and stepped in them. Then all I could see was some gray broken rock. On the other side of the rock, I couldn't see any footsteps at all. If I'd had anything left in my bladder, I would have wet myself.

I yelled back, "I've lost my tracks!"

James reassured me. "It should be OK. I think this area was cleaned but I can't be totally sure. You should be OK."

I yelled back, "*Should* is not good enough, James!"

He yelled back, "Do you have ***any*** idea of where you stepped next?"

I looked around and vaguely said, "Yes, kinda!" So I stepped carefully over to the rocks and then hopped onto one. About twenty feet in front of me, I could see my tracks again. Every step in the gap between the rocks and my tracks would be a risk. There was nothing to do but go for it and take as large steps onto the rocks as I could until I reconnected with my bootprints.

When I made it back to the group, James quietly pulled me aside. In a strong Scottish accent he whispered, "Shit, man, you should ha' told me you had to take a piss. I would ha' given you a bottle to piss in. No one wanders out there."

My heart still racing, I thanked him. He then spoke loud enough for everyone to hear. "This place is crazy. There are minefields all the way from Suez hundreds of miles south. They ha' ne'er been able to map them all. With the shifting sands, we just don't know where they all are from one day to the next."

Mines were part of life in this area. I had forgotten how people almost took for granted that everyone knew of the danger. I was still pretty much a naïve Canadian on assignment. Even though I had heard a lot of mines exploding on my previous visit to Hurghuda, this was way too close for comfort.

Hesham, our local Egyptian oceanographer, and I had spent a few months the year before in 1985 setting things up to do environmental surveys along the coast from Suez to the small town of Hurghada 250 miles south. We conducted arial reconnaissance, flying with a helicopter service company called Petroleum Air Services out of a base in Ras Gharib. Jonny, a large, brash American fellow, was our hardened ex-Vietnam pilot. He had obviously seen a lot of action and had not been not fazed by being hit by enemy fire more than once in southeast Asia.

When we initially met, Jonny's first words betrayed his southern U.S. origins. "What the heck are y'all doing way the fuck in the middle of noplace? I hear you guys are doing some environmental work." When I replied "yup", he put his huge hand on my shoulder, stared me straight in the eye and launched into a monologue, probably the most sentences I would ever hear him string together at once.

"Boys, I know what you are doin' seems like a damn good idea. But ya really think that anyone gives a fuck! We are so far from noplace. The oil companies don't give a shit. Rigs and pipelines spill oil every day. In fact, it is a freaking constant ooze of oil directly into that Gulf. You think the suits in Cairo, Alexandria or Houston care? They're darn far away. Nobody sees this hell hole. They don't care. People in Cairo and Alex can't even feed themselves, so do you really think they care what is going on hundreds of miles away from their home way the fuck out here? You think suits in Houston care? As long as the oil is flowing, that is all that matters. Look, I've been told by higher ups to take you guys on a 'tour', but I was instructed to take you only to certain areas...if ya know what I mean."

Jonny then turned and limped out of the hangar to a Bell 212 helicopter. Hesham and I followed. Jonny slid into the pilot's seat and Hesham jumped into the co-pilot's seat. Jonny gave him a dirty look and said, "No, no. You, my friend, in the back. The kid sits up front with me."

I felt bad for Hesham, but I needed to get some good arial shots. I climbed in, buckled up and looked to Jonny. He gestured to his headset, pointed at mine and gestured to me to do the same. As he started the rotors, I heard him say through the radio, "Now we can talk. OK, kid. Get your camera set between your legs and be ready to shoot through the glass at your feet." I nodded.

The rotors roared as we lifted off and headed out into the Gulf of Suez, leaving behind visions of the contaminated shoreline. On the approaching horizon, we could see hundreds of oil rigs with black smoke billowing from each of their flares. "I want to show you something," Jonny said.

Jonny approached an unmanned rig that was slowly pumping oil. There was no flare burning off this one, so we landed on a small helipad. As we walked around on the upper deck all we could hear was the clunking of an over-used pump. The smell of oil filled the air.

"Take a look down there," Jonny said, pointing to the water underneath the rig. Oil was seeping up from the sea floor. "Take a photo of that. Broken pipe. Nobody does any maintenance 'round here."

I started shooting.

With the whir of the rotors, we took off again, passing low over another rig. The fallout from its flare coated our windshield with specks of oil.

We flew for quite some time like this, me taking tons of photos and Hesham sitting silent in the back. Then Jonny changed direction away from the Gulf and flew us back over Ras Gharib out into the desert.

"Where the heck are we going?", I asked him.

"I want to show you something..." he replied, pointing with his chin towards the horizon. Following his gaze westward, I thought I saw a lake shimmering in the distance.

Now what is a lake doing way out in the middle of the desert?

As we got closer, I could see the lake was actually black. Jonny filled me in over the headset. "That lake of oil is probably ten miles long by five miles wide. And it's all from a pipeline rupture that happened three months ago. The break is still spewing oil and the lake grows more each day...."

I couldn't believe a rupture that had happened that long ago had not yet been stopped. I must have looked amazed because he said, "I told ya. No one gives a shit." Coming from someone who'd flown "too long" in 'Nam and seen everything, his words and these images really hit me hard.

As we headed back to base, Jonny shared with me that he lived in Germany and alternated four week stints in the Gulf, then four weeks off at home. In his words, "This is a shit hole...but the money is good."

What I saw the next day made the "shit hole" look like a picnic. On this "tour", we were going to transport two oil execs between company facilities. As we powered up, Jonny opened our private headset dialogue again. He told me to keep my camera down between my legs and to not let anyone see it while we were flying over some areas "you won't believe". We headed over the Gulf of Suez directly to the Sinai Peninsula, passing Ras Muhammad and flying north along the coast. Below me through the glass, I could see rivers of oil flowing into the Gulf. We landed at a Petrobel facility and two Egyptian oil execs with a military bodyguard, complete with a machine gun, jumped in the back.

Jonny looked over at me with concern on his face. He gazed down toward my hidden camera.

We took off again, flying north. Underneath us was the worst thing I had ever seen. A pipeline had ruptured on the coast and a river of oil about a quarter mile wide was flowing right from the shore directly into the Gulf of Suez. I carefully lowered my camera into position and started banging off photos. Glancing over at Jonny, I could see he was trying not to be conspicuous to the guests in the back as he maneuvered our flight path to give me the best views of the horror below. We both knew that if anyone in the back saw what we were doing that we both could be imprisoned for spying. We continued on past that river of black ooze. Everywhere we looked, oil coated the coastline. I took as many photos as I could before we landed at the second company facility and let the others get out.

At one point on our way back to Ras Gharib, Jonny glanced at me and said, "Nigel, you need to get these photos back and let people know what is going on out here."

Before I opened the latch to jump out of the chopper, I looked Jonny straight in the eye. We had just spent the last week together, sharing what few people in the world knew existed. I thanked him. He winked and mouthed back the words, "No, kid. Thank you!"

Hesham had our car waiting for me. As we pulled out of Ras Gharib, the sight of those flares burning in the distance, the oil washing on the shore and Jonny heading into the air again haunted me. I kept wondering if his comment that no one cared was right...or if it was a matter of the people who did know only cared about their large oil company bonuses.

I decided I really needed to also see what was happening below the surface of the Gulf. As a certified scuba diver, I could. So I headed back to the old Club Med in Hurghada to have a look at the nearby islands. We arrived late at night, this time to be greeted at the front desk by a beautiful dark-skinned French girl. I asked if they had a room for a few nights as I wanted to hire a boat and a dive guide to visit some of the offshore islands. Her English was not that good. My high school French was worse. She nodded her head and escorted me along a dark path to a small bungalow, where she opened up all the windows to allow the cool sea air to cleanse the room. She turned to me and held out her hand to pass me the room key. As she did so, she leaned forward and kissed me on the cheek while whispering, "Bon soir, Monsieur Nigel." I took a quick cool shower to wash off the grime from the day and quickly fell into a deep sleep.

Early the next morning, I woke to a knock at my door. Pierre, a Frenchman who had been raised in Taiwan, was to be my dive guide. His English was very unusual. I eventually got accustomed to the mix of Chinese and French in his accent. Grabbing a cheap Kodak underwater camera from the cute girl at the front desk, I headed out with Pierre and his colleague, Jacques, on a small boat. We were soon dropping anchor on the leeward side of our first island of investigation.

We checked each other's dive equipment before slowly descending through the calm, warm water. Some of the most amazing underwater life I had ever seen surrounded us. It was even more impressive than what I had watched as a kid on the popular TV series *The Undersea World of Jacques Cousteau*. The coral reefs were amazing, abundant with lion fish, massive groupers, small sharks and barracuda.

> *Can this be possible? The surface of the northern Gulf is extremely contaminated but down here it's like paradise...*

I wondered how this could be as I took pictures and teased Pierre into seeing how close we could get to a massive big-mouthed grouper. Eventually, we surfaced and climbed back up into the small dive boat and grabbed a bit of pita bread and a drink.

As Pierre gulped down his yogurt beverage, he said, "Nice, no?"

I nodded and said, "Oui, mon ami, *very* nice."

He smiled a warning at me, "Wait until après lunch...you will be surprised."

We finished the pita bread, hummus and a few olives and then pulled anchor to head around to the windward side of the island.

Pierre was right. I couldn't believe what I saw. The beach of the island was heavily polluted with garbage, plastic bottles, bags and those damn bird cages, of all things. I learned that the crew on oil tankers and fishing boats would keep live chickens in cages. Once they killed the birds to eat, they'd throw the cages overboard. Wherever the vessels were from, refrigeration must have been non-existent. The beaches throughout the area were littered with empty cages.

We dropped anchor, and I could taste the smell of pungent oil again. We geared up again and dropped into the sea, Pierre watching as we descended below the surface. What I saw was shocking. There were hardly any fish. The reef below was entirely bleached white. Oil and garbage were stuck all over the dead coral. Parts of the reef were shattered, for some mysterious reason I couldn't figure out. I took several photos and then gestured to Pierre to return topside. As I surfaced, I noticed a thin layer of oil coated my skin and my mask. I slipped climbing back into the boat from the black slime all over me.

This time it was Pierre's turn to challenge me. "Nigel, you need to do something. Oui, this is horrible. People come for vacation in dis small Magawish town, but we only take dem to the udder side of de island. La nice side. La side where de currents don't carry de oil. Every night, we 'ave to clean our own beach to take away all de garbage and tar ball. It gets worse and worse each month."

I stayed for a few more days, taking more pictures and wrestling with my thoughts. When I went to say goodbye to Pierre, I asked him where the French girl was as I also wanted to thank her. He smirked and told me she was down at the beach tending to a boat. I walked down to where he directed me. As I approached, she turned. I almost stumbled in embarrassment: she was topless. I blushed and nervously thanked her for hosting me. We kissed cheeks and I muttered a faint "merci". She smiled warmly and softly said in a thick French accent, "You are welcome, Monsieur Nigel."

I hastily headed around the corner to find Hesham, who was waiting for me with the car. He showered me with questions. "Are you OK? Are you ready to go back to Alexandria?" For a moment, I hesitated before replying. "I was until about two minutes ago...but we have things to do, and I need to go back to Alex."

And with that, Hesham and I headed back to the city. As we made our way up the terrible coastal road, we could hear intermittent explosions in the distance. With each explosion, I wondered if someone had stepped on a mine. Then a few minutes later, I'd hear another.

Perhaps they've found a bunch of mines and are detonating them...

When we got closer to the coast, Hesham directed me to look out at two small boats. "They are fishing with dynamite," the oceanographer said. "They drop dynamite over the side. The explosion causes a compression wave that stuns all the fish in the area. The fish float to the surface and the boats simply go around and pick them all up with nets. What they don't know is that, besides taking out all the fish, they are also destroying the reefs that are their habitat."

Suddenly I understood what I had seen while diving on the leeward side of the island. The reef had been shattered by the fishermen's dynamite.

All of these images flooded my mind on the flight back to London. Many seeds of discontent and doubt had been planted in me. I wondered over and over what my father had been incarcerated for, whether it had to do with any of the things I had seen or something else entirely. It would be our CFO Clark and my sister Sue who would help me sort out the details of his story over the coming weeks and months.

While I was nervously resting safely in Britain, my father was being held in the Cairo jailhouse in a cell with fifty other men from all over southern Egypt and Sudan. They were crammed in so tightly that everyone had to stand. The front row nearest the door laid down in shifts to rest. In the back of the cell was an area where they urinated and shit. In 95-degree heat, the smell in this horrible place must have been overwhelming.

Day after day, my father was shackled hand and foot and taken out to a donkey-drawn wagon, which was basically a metal box, and crammed in with other inmates heading to see a judge. They were forced to wait in the wagon in the hot sun until finally being taken back to their cells in the late afternoon. This went on for a week or so until one day he was taken out of the wagon and marched up to the courtroom. A judge announced, "You are guilty of corruption of a government official and, according to Sharia law, **you are guilty until proven innocent**." My father was then marched back to the wagon, where he fell down in great pain and passed a kidney stone from dehydration.

Night after night and day after day, he was held in the packed cell. Only one man spoke any English, a member of the Palestine Liberation Organization. He also spoke Arabic and helped my father by getting him food and giving him advice. Back then in Egypt, people in jail were not fed by the authorities. You had to have people from the outside bring you food if you were to survive.

After a few weeks in these horrible conditions, a doctor finally came from the Canadian Embassy to check on his health. My father told him that if he had to stay there any longer, he would surely die. The doctor did what he could to help. He told my father in confidence, "It takes me approximately ten minutes to get out of the jail system. So please wait for about eight minutes and then fake a heart attack. They will have to find me and I will come back and look you over. Then I can get you to the infirmary."

So that's what they did to get my father placed under the doctor's care. The infirmary was actually part of the jail asylum, so my father was surrounded by extremely unstable men, perhaps driven that way from the conditions under which they were living. Apparently, they would throw their own shit at each other, often hitting my dad in the crossfire.

My father was held here for quite some time. When he was deemed better, they started dragging him back to the waiting room in the courthouse each day. This back and forth went on for months without him ever seeing a judge. Through the Consul, he eventually heard that a major sting operation had gone down and that the police had grabbed many visiting CEOs and directors of international companies. He also heard that a Japanese CEO had recently died from the horrendous conditions.

CHAPTER 3
Breaking Away

I remember landing back in Vancouver after fleeing Cairo, being seated at the back of the aircraft yet again and having to wait for everyone to get their carry-on bags down from the overhead bins and slowly move off the 747. The process took so long it was killing me. By the time I finally reached the gangway, I almost dropped to my knees to kiss the ground.

My girlfriend Rieko had arranged to meet me at the airport. I made my way through customs to the baggage claim area, where it seemed like it took forever for my bag to show up. When it finally did come down the chute, it hit the side of the carousel and exploded, spewing my belongings all over the conveyor and the floor.

What next?

I pushed my way through to the front of the crowd, grabbed my suitcase and began shoving my stuff into it. The fiberglass exterior had obviously been damaged and then taped back up again.

Had the Egyptians broken open my suitcase and looked through it?

I would never know. I piled all my stuff onto a trolley and pushed it past the last customs check towards the waiting crowd.

As soon as I got through the door, I began searching for Rieko. When her eyes met mine, I could see we both were crying. I forced my way through the crowd.

I'll never forget that hug, the first since departing Vancouver so many months before. I could have stood there with her in the middle of a busy airport forever. But we had things to do. We jumped into her father's old rusted Nissan and drove straight downtown to the company office on Pender Street at Thurlow.

I skipped the elevator and chose the stairs. Grabbing the doorknob to the cold concrete stairwell, I was very aware of what I had to do. My father's company had leased the entire second floor and sublet a few spots to help pay the rent. As I walked into the section that was our office, I saw my sister Sue waiting for me at the elevator doors. I came up behind her and quietly said, "Hi, Sue." She turned around and, although she never swears, her first words to me were, "What the *fuck* is going on?"

The rest of the staff quickly gathered round us. I told everyone that my father was in jail in Egypt and, seeing their disbelief and shock, told them that things were dire but we had it all under control. Sue and I stepped into her office and closed the door. We stayed in there for hours, talking about what was happening and trying to figure out a plan. We really had no idea what to do next.

Our family business really *was* in dire straights. All invoices related to the Egyptian project were frozen. Our joint venture in Brazil was suing us.

The situation was very difficult for Sue and me to navigate. Although Sue had graduated with a degree in outdoor recreation from Simon Fraser University, my father had hired her to work as a bookkeeper in his business in the early days. I had been working on and off, primarily overseas, for him since I was sixteen. This was the man who had helped me set up my own business, called Aqua-Guard Sales, in high school. I would go door to door with a buddy and ask to measure people's swimming pools, then buy the raw material and cut a pool cover to fit. I started importing small pumps from China that would help boat owners do an oil change without having to take the boat out of the water. My father, ever the businessman, encouraged me to explore these and other entrepreneurial ideas I had.

But nothing during our years of growing up had prepared us for what was happening now. We both seriously questioned what was going on with my father. I held him on a very high pedestal and thought no one could knock him off. Sue had been having issues with my father while I was away, but I wouldn't find out what those were or the details until a decade later.

So, in spite of everything, Sue and I decided to do what we could to hold my dad's company together. The workload was daunting: we found ourselves putting in long hours during the week, plus weekends and evenings.

During all this time, Sue and I kept working to get our father freed from prison. We spent many, many hours at the offices of our Members of Parliament, trying to get some action on the diplomatic front. We talked about angles the federal government of Canada could use to get my father back. Unfortunately, we were left with the sense that most of our attempts fell on deaf ears.

During this period, I really began to question my upbringing. I started to understand that everyone evolves with their own set of core values, influenced in part by their life experiences. As the story of my father started to slowly unravel, I could see that he had a different set of core values from me. He grew up in Britain during WWII under very difficult circumstances. He had joined the merchant navy as a chief engineer and spent five years traveling from the United Kingdom to South America and up the coast of North America to Alaska, picking up and dropping off goods and British mail. In 1966, he had courageously left Newport, Wales, where I and my two sisters had been born, to start a new life. All he had with him when he left the old country were a few wooden crates filled with our meager possessions, his street smarts and his determination. He was driven to succeed at all costs.

He bravely loaded his young family onto the *Hanseatic*, a people mover ship sailing from Southampton to Halifax on Canada's east coast. We arrived in the new land on June 1st 1966. My father had lined up a job to support his wife and three very young children on Canada's west coast, so we had to make our way across the country to Port Alice on the tip of Vancouver Island. We lived in Port Alice for two rainy years, the mud coming up to our knees at times, until the day my father started a pressure washing business in Vancouver. For a few years, he rented whatever housing he could afford until he had enough for a down payment on a small home in a remote section of the city that only had access via a dirt road. I ended up attending high school with mostly immigrants and second generationers from the U.K. and Germany.

In 1968, my dad and a friend took an old truck and a pressure washer down to Santa Barbara, California to help fight a massive oil spill. With the money he made cleaning beaches, he founded a startup in Vancouver called Bennett Pollution Controls. The company fabricated oil containment barriers and occasionally sent teams around the world to fight spills. At the age of 40, he sold this company and invested 90% of the proceeds into a land development scheme in Maui. That project went bust and he was forced to go back to work. So he founded Bennett Environmental Consultants Ltd. with a focus on producing oil spill contingency plans for governments and entire countries. Over the years, my father seemed to be caught up in a cycle of making money and losing it. Through it all, it looked to me as if his #1 goal was to make it big. Perhaps if he had been raised in a different era or under different circumstances, things would have been different. But he hadn't been.

When my father was in prison in Egypt, I had not been dating Rieko for very long. She, unlike him, was not motivated by money or glamour. The instant my good buddy Dmac (Dave McDonald) and his girlfriend introduced me to this beautiful, funny, intelligent and adventurous woman, we got along. She had been born in a tiny fishing village in southern Japan, three hours from Hiroshima by train. Her father Kunio, another true adventurer, had spent years away from his family, learning Spanish from his Mexican friends while working as a picker on farms in southern California.

When Rieko was four, Kunio moved his wife and two children from Japan to a ranch near a small remote town in Alberta, Canada. The four of them lived in a long house with 20 other families for a bitterly cold, long year while he worked as a ranch hand. Rieko's mother originally thought she was leaving her tiny village in Japan for the promised land. But their new life in rural Alberta turned out to be hell. The work was hard. The weather even worse. There was only one outhouse for everyone and it was 100 yards out in the field. She cried every night for months on end. Eventually, Kunio moved them all to a tiny basement suite in a home in Vancouver. The owner, an older woman, had offered the family lodging in exchange for help. Kunio started a gardening service to earn some income. A kind and simple man, he eventually became the vice president of the Vancouver Buddhist Church.

I knew Rieko was special. We balanced each other perfectly, kind of like yin and yang. This woman, no stranger to hard work and a recent university graduate in primary education, had good family values. And she was willing to put up with me and my ADD and dyslexia.

In late 1988, my father was released from the prison infirmary into house arrest in a local hotel in Cairo. My mother joined him there. After several months, our controller Clark went to Cairo as well to see if he could help garner my father's full release. The two of them decided that things did not look good and that my father would either die or spend the rest of his life in an Egyptian jail. So Clark decided to try a dry run of an escape. He took a tour bus to the border with Israel to see how difficult it would be to pass. He counted the number of military check points, including how many times anyone would have to show their passport before they could enter Israel. He went the entire way and reported back that it could be possible.

The problem was my father no longer had his passport: the police had taken it. So Clark had a friend's passport doctored with a new photo of a similar-looking Caucasian man with silver gray hair. They assumed that if my father traveled with my mother, they would not be as suspicious. They also assumed that the hotel room was bugged. So each night my father and mother would plan the details of their escape under the bed sheets, as it was the only place in their room where they figured they could not be heard.

And then the day came for them to make their escape. They left their room and nonchalantly took the elevator down to the hotel lobby to join their tour bus to Israel. But as soon as the elevator doors opened, they realized their plan was doomed. The entire bus was already being loaded with Orthodox Jews with their black hats and long sidelocks. My clean-shaven father and his wife would stick out like a sore thumb. In shock, they slowly turned around and went back to their room.

They looked for another bus tour to join, but there was nothing scheduled for a couple of weeks. While they waited, my father was dragged back and forth to the court with his Egyptian lawyer, who had become a good ally and friend. The judges told the lawyer that they had all the evidence they needed, including video and voice recordings and a confession from the deputy minister in question.

Then one day a policeman stormed into my father's hotel room, handcuffed him and dragged him to the court. Thinking this was the end and that he was heading for a life in an Egyptian prison, my father stepped in front of the judge expecting the worst. And then the judge said a few words in Arabic, which his lawyer translated as "You are free to go."

Within minutes, the lawyer whisked my father away to the hotel, where they picked up my mother and their few belongings, and then headed straight for the Cairo airport. Within a few hours, both of my parents were boarding the first plane they could get on that was heading out of the country. They made their way back to Vancouver via Europe.

Later we found out that the deputy minister who was the key witness in the case against my father had died of a heart attack in prison, and so the authorities had to drop the charges against all the executives he had incriminated who were still being held. That news came too late for the one Japanese executive who had died while waiting in jail.

When my father arrived back in the office in Vancouver at the beginning of 1989, he acted as if nothing had happened. A perfect example of that old British saying, "Keep calm and carry on."

Soon after his return, one of the largest oil spills in history hit the mainstream news. On March 24th 1989, an Exxon Valdez super tanker carrying 55 million gallons of crude oil hit Bligh Reef in Alaska. Millions of gallons of oil started spilling directly into the pristine waters of Prince William Sound. Images of the beaches coated in black ooze, of oiled birds and seals were everywhere in the media. Our pristine final frontier had been violated by Big Oil.

Suddenly oil spills were not something just being talked about behind closed doors in remote regions of the world. They were happening here, right in North America's backyard, and people everywhere were angry.

Our office phone was ringing off the hook with TV channels requesting news interviews and participation in panel discussions. My father's company was technically in the oil spill **contingency planning** business and didn't really focus on oil spill **response** work. However, understanding the specific needs of our international clients and the overall need for better oil spill response technology, we had formed a joint venture manufacturing company in Sao Paulo, Brazil in 1982. A team, headed up by LP and myself, had been sent there to build oil spill containment barriers, skimming systems and boats. These products had all been intended for the Brazilian market and our one Egyptian project. But at the time of the Exxon Valdez spill, we had no equipment available in North America to help.

After the Exxon Valdez spill, we were awarded a major contract in Alaska to rewrite the entire marine oil spill contingency plans for the state. Over the next few years, the team at Bennett Environmental Consultants ramped up and we ended up reviewing and rewriting over 250 plans for the state of Alaska.

While that contract was good news, the unease I had been feeling about the mess in our environment now began to be matched by my unease about being in business with my father. I didn't like always being in survival mode with everything constantly around me going sideways. I swore that I would never let myself be put in a situation like Egypt ever again. Not that I never wanted to travel again. I just didn't want to be constantly operating in crisis mode as my father had before me.

Everyone has their struggles: everyone has skeletons in their closet. My skeleton, as I was starting to understand, just happened to be my father.

I was determined to live by my own values—not my father's. As the dust started to settle from the Egyptian ordeal and the Exxon Valdez oil spill, my sister Sue, my friend LP and I began resuscitating my old company. Aqua-Guard Sales emerged as Aqua-Guard Technologies. Our new business was focused on manufacturing oil spill recovery equipment in Canada. For the next two years, we three spent all our weekdays working full-time for my father and all our nights and weekends getting Aqua-Guard off the ground. Gradually, we set up a network of sub-manufacturers that could build our oil containment barriers and small oil skimming systems to our designs. An act of environmental terrorism pushed us to think about what was next.

When Saddam Hussein invaded Kuwait in August 1990, he blew up most of the country's oil infrastructure, causing huge fires in the desert and massive oil spills in the Persian Gulf. Saudi Aramco contacted us for assistance and, in the end, purchased our small stockpile of oil spill containment barriers. We flew them direct to the Gulf to help in the response efforts. It was like we were replaying the Exxon Valdez all over again: we didn't have enough equipment to really help much. I was reminded of what pilot Jonny had said and, unlike in Egypt and Venezuela prior, people were now actually beginning to "give a shit". That knowledge spurred us on to look for new opportunities.

The work schedule we had was exhausting. Not only that, but the ethical issues that Sue and I had with my father were growing more apparent. We were stressed and exhausted.

We needed to somehow get away from it all.

I don't know if it was our obsession with adventure that had us turn to the outdoors. Maybe it was because escaping from the office and society in general to head into Nature gave me time and space to think—even if just for brief moments. I do know I just loved the sense of freedom I felt while outside. When I was a teenager, I would head off alone into the mountains, climb to the top of a peak and sit and contemplate. That's where I felt comfortable questioning who I was and why everyone else in my class seemed smarter than me. For me, doing something physical outdoors had always been the best way to cope with everything in life.

Whatever the reason, when work got really intense, Sue and I would spend as much time as we could testing ourselves physically. Mountaineering, skiing, scuba diving, mountain bike racing, sailboat racing: you name it, we'd do it if it pushed our limits. After riding her bike across Canada a few years before, Sue had turned to more extreme mountain sports. She knew I was afraid of heights, and so she dragged me into taking a rock-climbing course through the Federation of Mountain Clubs of British Columbia. Soon we both became addicted to climbing. There were no climbing walls back then, so we would take off for the granite cliffs of Squamish every free moment we had. Usually Sue's boyfriend Ken Legg, a highly accomplished climber and backcountry skier, would lead us.

Over the years, we became addicted to pushing our limits during our time off. Addicted to taking risks. If a chasm opened in front of us, we wouldn't hesitate before taking a leap. Ken caught a great photo of me doing just that (yes, that's me on the front cover) when we bagged the summit of Mount Baker in Washington State together. As young entrepreneurs, Sue and I didn't yet know that we'd be doing the same thing—pushing our limits and taking leap after leap—in our business.

In winter, we would change gears and head to the mountains with our skis. I had skied downhill since I was very young, but backcountry skiing was new to me. In the winter of 1989, Sue and Ken announced they would take me with them to a remote area called Overseer that December for a two-week trip. A helicopter would drop us near a small mountain hut that would be a base camp from which we could yoyo up and down, climbing some mountains and telemarking up and then skiing off the tops of others.

My first question to Ken was, "What the heck is telemarking?"

He told me, "Telemark skis are thin with metal edges and the bindings leave the heel of the boot free. To climb mountains, you glue mole skins to the bottom of the skis. Don't worry. Sue and I will build an 'up' track by compressing the snow and you can follow us. When we all get to the summit, we'll rip off the skins, point our skis down and drop off the top."

The summit of what? Where the heck was he taking us this time?

Always eager to try something different, I asked, "So when do we leave?"

"Next Saturday."

That gave me a whole week to rent the right gear, learn how to telemark and pack. Ken topped it all off with, "Oh, and we'll need a light tent to take with us as it will take two to three days to ski out once we're done."

A shiver of excitement went through me. At that point, I couldn't imagine how difficult it would be to telemark, performing deep knee bends on every turn with the weight of a large pack on our backs. At that point, I couldn't imagine how cold I might get. It was like none of that really mattered. I would deal with whatever happened. After all, nothing could be worse than our day-to-day business dealings.

Or so I thought.

When we arrived in Pemberton, a bitter coastal cold greeted us. Two other Swiss fellows joined Ken, Sue and myself for the helicopter trip into Overseer. When the chopper went to drop us at base camp, all we could see through the swirling snow which had been kicked up by the whirling rotor blades was a roof. This was the Harrison Hut, a small alpine shelter sitting at 5,700 feet above sea level. It would be our home for the next twelve days.

A snowstorm had hit the area a few days earlier, so as soon as we landed, we all had to work as a team and dig our way down through the snowpack to find the door. By the time we got enough snow moved away from the doorframe, I was already cold and eagerly grabbing the door handle to be the first to step inside.

One square room with a picnic table down the center, a potbelly stove, a stack of wood and a rudimentary steel sink. A loft where we would sleep side by side to keep warm. Hooks hanging down from the roof so we could stash our bags of food away from pack rats while we were out or sleeping. This was to be our temporary "home". Soon we were hunkered in for the night, toques on our heads and boots stashed inside our sleeping bags so they wouldn't freeze.

For the next few days, we awoke every morning to see our breath literally freezing in the air. We took turns being the one to stoke the fire, warm the hut and boil water for tea. Our plan was to summit as many peaks in the area as we could. The weather cooperated the first few days and we were able build a nice up track out from the hut.

The third night, however, a big weather system hit and dumped three feet of snow outside our door. Fresh powder posed no problem for Sue, who was a certified telemark instructor, or for Ken, who was a real mountain man and who had done some major climbs in the Himalayas and Peru. But I didn't have enough technique to be any good at telemarking with my rental skis. That, plus the training we did every morning in avalanche rescue techniques, made me a little uneasy setting out that morning. We climbed the up track past the tree line above the hut towards the open bowls on the way to bagging our first peak.

This region was amazing, with the massive Overseer peak looming at 9,019 feet overhead and both Zygo and Spidery on either side. After hours of careful trekking, we arrived at our first summit. Although I was grinning at the view, I

Sue & I - Coleman Glacier, USA (c1992)

was breathing heavier than I ever had, having switched on and off of the lead building up our new track. We shared a quick frozen snack, and then tore the climbing skins off our skis.

Ken pointed out a safe route down. "Stay over there on the mellower slope of the bowl. Don't head toward the steep areas over there and avoid there and there.... Everyone check to see your avalanche peeps are turned on and transmitting? And remember the avalanche training from this morning. OK then...." And with a sudden, "Tally ho!", he launched off the summit into the deep powder, floating effortlessly, making turns like a pro and traveling non-stop down the slope.

Sue looked at me, smiled, then yelled "Crampi Aligampi!" as she jumped off with the same skill and disappeared from view.

And now my moment of truth.

I took one last look at the amazingly blue sky and all the white peaks surrounding me. There was no one around for hundreds of miles. I took a deep breath and launched off the top. Within seconds, I was taking my first deep knee bend to force a compression turn. But my uphill ski flipped on its edge and, "Boom!" There I was, flying through the air and landing face first in this giant white pillow. Fresh snow jammed the cracks between my jacket and pants and clung to my neck.

OMG, this is freaking cold!

I rushed to get up, but my poles just sank in the deep snow. I struggled and struggled but couldn't get up. Ken and Sue were completely out of sight. Finally I got a good enough grasp on my poles to lift myself back to my feet.

This is going to be a ***long*** *two weeks!*

I looked down the slope to pick out my route again. This time I made three whole turns before crashing. The next, five turns. And the next, three. Each time I fell, I stayed calm and slowly got up. Within ten minutes, I was exhausted. By the time I finally got to where Sue and Ken were waiting for me, I was so stoked that I enthusiastically yelled out, "Hey, I linked five turns!" They both looked at each other and then laughed. Sue responded, "Pretty good for a first-timer. Aren't you beat from all that falling and getting up?"

I admitted, "I'm destroyed...but, wow, that was amazing. Let's do it again!" I'll never forget Sue's response: "Next time we will send you first. After all, you are the expendable brother!"

Thankfully, she was just joking. For that night, it snowed another two feet. As soon as I saw the fresh powder and the zero degree Fahrenheit temperature, I knew it was going to be a bitch creating an up track that morning. Ken took the lead, followed by Sue and the Swiss guys, with me bringing up the rear. The first 45 minutes were hell, but I didn't want to let the group know how tired I was from the day before. Soon they were way ahead of me, fast approaching the tree line.

And then something totally unanticipated happened. My stomach started to spasm. I had to take a shit. Like—now!

I can't go back to the hut. It's too far to go down and climb back up again. If I take off my skis, I'll sink. Maybe if I turn away from the slope and stick my skis in backwards, then I can pull my pants down...?

I repositioned myself, and tried to grab my pants and underwear to pull them down. But my semi-frozen hands were wrapped up with the poles and every move got me more tangled. A bit came out in my underwear. And a bit more. I could feel it against my skin...

Awwwww...this is not good.

Finally, I was able to get my pants down and do the rest of what I had to do in a small hole I made in the snow. Now the smell coming from my fully loaded underwear made me retch. My fingers were useless by now. So I bent down, grabbed the edge of my underwear with my teeth, and started to pull my head away quickly to tear the cloth. First one side ripped away, and then the other. After about ten minutes of struggling, I was able to tear my underwear right off, bury it, wipe what I had to wipe, and roughly wash my hands with snow.

This is ***not*** *a good start to the day. I'm exhausted. My ass is freezing. And I can see everyone's waiting for me at the top of the tree line now.*

I hustled as fast as I could. As I came up to the group, the two Swiss guys were just waving goodbye. They were going to attempt the summit of Overseer, which was to our right. We were planning to head up a smaller peak to the left. As they began to lay their fresh track, Ken yelled out a warning: "Be really careful! The avalanche danger is high." They soon disappeared, along with their ropes and ice equipment, along a ridge above us.

We began the climb to reach our peak by taking our skis off. In spots, the snow was sloughing off the mountain. In other spots, there was ice. Carefully kick stepping our way reduced the danger of sliding and we made it safely to the top. We looked across at Overseer and spotted the Swiss guys quite high up. After a bite of lunch, we pulled off our climbing skins again and dropped off the steep hill.

The ride down went smoother this time. By the time we were arriving back at the hut, it was just getting dark. Suddenly, the entire Overseer region was roaring with the fearsome sounds of falling ice and raging snow. We heard the cracking sound of an avalanche. We looked around to locate the slide, and saw it ripping down the main mountain at over 100 miles per hour, taking out everything in its path.

We looked at each other and then, all at the same time, together said, "The Swiss guys!" We looked at Overseer but could see nothing. The entire side of the mountain had let go. We rushed into the hut and began to grab up our gear and our headlamps, thinking that a rescue or, God forbid, a recovery was in order. And then we heard voices coming over the ridge. We opened the door of the hut to see a faint light zigzagging its way towards us. It was the Swiss guys, chatting as they skied down the last bit of the slope. The first words they uttered coming through the door were a shaky, "Happy New Year!"

We had forgotten it was New Year's Eve, but they hadn't. They pulled out their "secret" schnapps and began celebrating being alive. They were pretty quiet for a while, reflecting, I supposed, on what could have happened. As the schnapps kicked in, they started to chuckle nervously and then they began to share their story.

Apparently, our Swiss colleagues had seen chunks of ice starting to fall and so had turned back just in time. Fortunately, the avalanche had taken a different route and passed them by. Over the next ten years, Sue and I would have nine friends and acquaintances die in avalanches around British Columbia and Alaska.

To cut through the nervousness hanging over the group, I told them the story about my situation earlier in the day. Ken instantly grabbed the uncooked tortellini I had in my hands and told me to sit down. Apparently, it was not going to be my turn to cook dinner that night.

Over the next week, my telemarking skills improved. By the time we had to leave, I was really enjoying crazily trekking up to a peak, ripping off my skins and linking turns on the ski down like the rest of them. Well, maybe not as good as the rest of them. But as good as I needed to be to enjoy myself.

And then the day came for Sue, Ken and I to begin our trek back to civilization. The Swiss had headed out the day before. We three dressed for the record-breaking minus four degrees Fahrenheit weather and loaded up our 50-pound packs. For the first few hours, it was like moving through a Christmas wonderland. But gradually, the healthy trees and pristine slopes turned into a wasteland of windfall. We were climbing over downed trees, taking off our packs to slide under downed trees, getting caught in branches of downed trees. It was like trying to make our way through a minefield. With no time and too cold to stop and eat, we snacked our way through until we reached a spot where the snow was literally covered in fallen trees.

Ken stopped and said, "Shit, we're lost! The access road from Meager Creek should be here somewhere. But it's late and starting to get dark. We may have to spend the night in this hell hole."

This is going to be one cold and uncomfortable night....

Ken offered to do a recon. And so for about thirty minutes, Sue and I huddled together, shivering. We had told Ken's parents to expect us at their cabin on Green Lake at Whistler that night or the next, and they would probably be worried if we were late. When Ken got back, he reassured us that the logging road was here...somewhere...and that it would be better if we kept moving. All we had were a topographical map and a compass—no GPS or cell phone apps in those days. So we donned our headlamps, hauled on our beastly backpacks, and started working our way through the hell field again. At midnight, we hit a clearing and followed Ken's instincts to head downhill.

It was then we found the snow-covered logging road. Fifteen miles from our destination. And it was getting even colder. So we began to run on our skis to keep warm. After about 45 minutes of running, we spotted mist rising off the Meager Creek Hot Springs. Cold and dirty after 12 days without a shower, we dropped our packs and clothes beside the hot springs and jumped in. We sat in the warm water for an hour, laughing as our muscles seized up from exhaustion and talking about the food we would eat when we got out of this place. But we couldn't stay in the natural hot tub forever. Our flesh would melt off our bones and we would turn into soup. Someone had to jump out into the snow, butt naked and bare footed, and grab our clothes. We drew straws and the expendable brother lost.

I jumped out and ran to where we had left our packs—but there was nothing there. Or at least I couldn't see anything at first. As my eyes adjusted, I realized that our clothes were covered in a thick frost from the mist coming off the hot springs. I grabbed my underwear. They were solid. I shook them, but no good.

Shit! How am I going to get my clothes on? What can break this ice?

A tree...yes, I had to smash my underwear on a tree so I could loosen the ice before pulling them on.

Fuck, it's cold!

The same thing for the rest of my clothes...my socks, shirt, and jacket. Worst of all were my blister-creating boots. They were solid and there was nothing I could do to warm them up or soften their killing edges. I pulled them on, ran around for thirty seconds, then grabbed my backpack before heading over to tell Ken and Sue about their frozen clothes.

As I waited for them to do their own dance of getting dressed, I took my gloves off and tried to tie a small, empty can of gas back onto my pack. My fingers were screaming in pain from the onset of frostbite. And I was shivering non-stop from the cold. So I announced that I had to get moving and that I'd head down the road ahead of them to warm up. I took off, slowly slugging my way along the rough flat surface, until they finally caught up with me. Ken told us if we didn't stop now we would die. We stopped for a moment, shuffling our feet back and forth, grunting, trying to figure out what to do in the minus 13 degree dark. We were out of fuel. We were out of food, save for a few chocolates. But we had our sleeping bags and a tent. So we decided to pitch it in the middle of the road and try to get some sleep.

Sue and Ken got the tent up and zipped their bags together for warmth. I slid into my sleeping bag with everything on but my boots. They zipped it closed around me, leaving just enough room for me to breath and catch the few chocolate rose buds they fed me through the gap. An hour later, some drunk yahoos on a snowmobile almost crashed through our tent. They came roaring up the road on their way to the hot springs and, at the last second, we three all rolled together to the side of the tent. We didn't know if they were ever coming back our way. It was too cold to move the tent. We couldn't get back to sleep. So we just huddled together, waiting out the night.

When daylight finally appeared, Sue quietly asked, "Nigel, are you alive?"

I groaned in reply. We put on our frozen boots, took down the tent and skied off down the road. I kept praying for a slope so we could ski downhill, but it never came. And then we heard the most welcome sound in the world: a car trying to negotiate the road ahead of us. We flagged it down and asked for help. They only had space for one person—and I was voted to be the one in worst condition—so I climbed in and headed back to town with them, glad for the warmth of their vehicle.

I found my old 1980 Volvo where we'd parked it twelve days before, covered in several feet of snow. It took forever to dig it out. But there was a heater inside that worked, so I took off back up Meager Creek Hot Springs Road to meet up with Sue and Ken, all the while my hands screaming in pain as they thawed out. I found them, looking tired and cold, still skiing their way out. We all hugged, piled into the car and headed for the cabin on Green Lake.

As we pulled ourselves out of the Volvo, we could smell wood burning on the fireplace and see smoke rising from the chimney into the blue sky. The car's heavy steel doors closed with a "thunk" in the muffled silence of the wintry landscape. The frozen lake in front of us was serene. It was a picture perfect moment.

Ken's parents cheerfully greeted us from where they sat by the fireplace with a "Happy New Year!" But when they turned to see us coming into the room, we could see the shock on their faces. "Wow, what happened to you guys? You look like you've been through the wringer. We were very close to calling Search and Rescue. Do you realize that was the coldest spell we have had in years?"

We looked at each other. Ken and Sue's lips were all chapped and their skin was raw from exposure. My hands were still throbbing as they thawed. We could feel the warmth of the fire and the aroma of cooking filled the air.

> *What a crazy adventure this has been. I was almost dead. And yet, at the same time, I have never felt so alive and so invigorated.*

I looked over at Ken and asked, "So where are you dragging me to next?"

We all laughed.

This particular weekend, Rieko, our friends Jeff, Ken and I were going to try to summit Sky Pilot again. Sky Pilot is a pointed peak 6,663 feet high, located near Squamish off the Sea-to-Sky highway between Vancouver and Whistler. It has quite a drop off on each side of the summit. The plan this weekend was to push up a different route than we had taken on our previous three attempts—all of which were unsuccessful. We would make our way over rocks and an ice field before entering a rock chimney and working our way up to the summit. Hopefully, Search and Rescue wouldn't have to come looking for us this time.

We used crampons, ice axes and ropes to make our way up the ice/snow slope onto the rock terrain from which we could make the final push for the summit. By the time we reached the scramble, the day was getting late. So the crew decided not to rope up, but to free climb from where we were on the loose rock face to the peak.

I froze to the rock. Although we were only 165 feet from the summit, the distance looked insurmountable to me. The exposure was high. My vertigo had kicked in and my knees were visibly shaking at the thought of having to step off a ledge into this particularly dodgy rock chimney. Once in the chimney, we would have to scramble up a steep incline over loose rock to the summit. The thought that stopped me from moving was that, after we stepped into the chimney, it opened out and dropped thousands of feet straight to the valley floor. Even though we had all been in some pretty crazy life-threatening situations before, this was not a risk I was willing to take. Perhaps it was a warning from the powers that be. Putting my life and Rieko's life in jeopardy by not roping up was not an option. It was one of those moments in which pushing things back inside my risk limit seemed the wisest thing to do.

I nervously raised my voice to the others. "If we are not roping up, I am not going. It's just too risky."

I totally understood that Jeff and Ken wanted to push on. This was our third attempt to climb Sky Pilot. But they had not been hit with the vertigo I was dealing with at this extreme exposure. They asked me, "Are you sure we can see the summit from here?". Rieko, who wasn't aware I was suffering, suggested we could both wait on an exposed ledge until they returned so we could all head back down the snow/ice wall together. We all agreed and Ken and Jeff pushed on.

It was getting late when they got back to us. We all high fived and, with one last glance toward the summit, we started to move down the mountain. Climbing down, in many cases, is more difficult than climbing up. This was one of those cases. With time pressing and none of us roped up, Jeff and Ken decided to move further over to the right side of the ice field to run a parallel route to us down the mountain. Rieko and I decided to stay more central and to kick step down the ice and snow in front of her. With my antiquated crampons, I decided to start out slowly. Directly below us was a field of boulders. If we slipped, we would slide straight down to them and be cut to pieces.

Rieko was following in my steps, about 25 yards above me, using her ice axe as an extra anchor. Suddenly, I heard a yelp. I looked up to see her speeding my way at about 50 miles an hour.

> *Oh shit! This is it...maybe I can catch her...no, she is going to hit me and we* ***both*** *will go careening down the slope into the boulders below....*

I braced myself for the impact...but nothing happened. I looked up to see that Rieko had fallen into a crevasse and abruptly stopped.

> *I can't believe this...we both should be dead.*

Time slowed down. I could see Rieko stuck in the crevasse up to her waist. I had no idea what was below her. It could be a giant cavern or just a small crack in the glacier. If she fell through without a rope, we might never be able to find her. Or she might fall 300 feet to the unimaginable.

Everything seemed to slow down and come into hyper focus for me. I knew exactly what I had to do.

I told her not to move. I passed her a rope and told her to tie off. Slowly, I crept up to where she was. Then I fixed an anchor in the snow with my ice axe and slowly, ever so slowly, I pulled her out.

We moved more to the left of the slope toward some rock patches to get off the ice and snow before we continued our climb down. After a few hours of hiking through the bush, we were finally safe in camp. It didn't matter that we had made another failed attempt on Sky Pilot. What mattered was that someone was looking out for us on the mountain that day. Again, I had been slapped back into reality.

I remember Rieko repeatedly saying to me that evening, "You are so lucky I didn't die on this trip—as my father would have killed you." Never mind what her father would have done to me. Losing her was a risk I couldn't—and didn't want to—take.

The biggest risk I *did* want to take was with Aqua-Guard. Sue and I were desperately looking for a change in our situation. So was LP. We knew we had a business that we could take international. We just didn't know how or when.

Each time we had an extreme adventure outdoors, we slipped back into our day-to-day living with little fanfare. But I was secretly stuck in survival mode.

I knew from experience that, when everything was on the line, I could focus intensely on what needed to get done. Over the next decade, intensity became my perceived normal. I came to realize that I operate well in this environment, moving from intense work in business to intense extremes outdoors. For a long time, I actually thought everyone operated this way.

By chance, in late 1991 an opportunity opened up in front of us. The Business Development Bank of Canada (BDC) showed up with an offer to evaluate our company and help us with a strategic plan. All my schooling had been technical. And none of us knew much about international business, just what we had learned during our travels (which actually panned out to be better than any formal education we could have paid for). This was the kind of advice we needed. After assessing the potential in our business, the BDC offered to pay half of the consulting costs if we agreed to act on whatever decisions came out of the strategic planning.

We discussed BDC's offer with our father, but he was quite strongly against using any outside help at all. He didn't trust others and had always believed in succeeding alone. Not trusting was my father's way of operating. It certainly wasn't a reflection of our values at Aqua-Guard. I had grown up knowing that I had to trust others to help me with things I had trouble with, like accounting. Sue and I both believed that no one succeeds alone and that no one person can be the expert in everything. That was part of Aqua-Guard's strength as a business. Sue and LP and I were a solid team: we filled in each other's gaps in a way that made us stronger than we would be on our own.

And so we chose differently than my father had. We went back to the team from BDC and agreed to take them on. All work would be done after hours and on the weekends. For the next six months, they coached us part-time. As the weeks wore on, it became increasingly clear to everyone that we three needed to break off from our father's company, form our own and focus on what we all did best.

I drew the short straw—again.

So one crisp and cool day in December 1992, I took a deep breath, marched into my father's office in downtown Vancouver and gingerly closed the door. A full head of silver white hair was the first thing that greeted me. His six-foot frame, intimidating and handsome even when seated, was bent over his desk. I told him that Sue, LP and I had decided to leave his company so we could run with Aqua-Guard. His face went entirely white and he didn't say a thing at first. He was *not* happy. What he did say when he eventually spoke shocked me.

"Fine. But you guys owe me."

I was taken aback and asked him, "What do we owe you? We've worked *for* you for years...."

He didn't answer me right away. But the next afternoon, he sternly walked into my office and dropped a piece of paper on my desk, saying, "This is what you owe me." It was a fairly large number, considering we had no assets and no cash flow. But we wanted out. What could we do but agree? So we signed a release with an IOU, closed the doors to our offices, and left the downtown tower for the last time.

CHAPTER 4
The Doorknob Effect

Leaving my father's downtown office that afternoon in 1992 was like leaving school on the last day. It felt surreal and, at the same, joyously inevitable.

> *Wow, we are actually doing this. We are going out on our own. At least now we'll have the freedom and energy to give everything to our new business.*

We had no idea what we were doing or where we were headed. But we did have a fair amount of experience in oil spill response planning, along with design and manufacturing experience from my father's Brazil operation. We re-incorporated the name Aqua-Guard one more time and called our new "start-up" Aqua-Guard Spill Response Inc.

I was learning more about the value of surrounding myself with good people, people who had expertise in areas I didn't and whom I could work with together as a team. I had first learned the importance of this the hard way back in school. I am dyslexic. In order to get through the education system, I had had to rely on a network of people who were smarter than me. This childhood survival strategy turned out to be just as valuable in my working life.

At Aqua-Guard, each of us had very different strengths. We three were the perfect blend of personalities for a startup. I was sociable and technically passable. Sue was a management and money organizer extraordinaire. LP was a technical genius. I did the sales and marketing for the business, Sue ran the operations, and LP came up with the visionary mechanical designs. Like Jim Collins said in his bestseller *Good to Great**, if our business had been a bus, we had put the perfect people in the right seats. The only thing was, when it came to driving, we worked as a tight collective, rather than as three separate solo bus drivers.

We looked all over Vancouver's Lower Mainland for a place to set up operations. Since we would be spending most of our waking hours at work, we wanted to find a place fairly close to where we all lived on Vancouver's "North Shore". We finally ended up signing a three-year lease on a 2,300-square-foot warehouse in North Vancouver itself that had a tiny front office.

Next up was our home. For the first three years of our marriage, Rieko had worked three jobs so we could save up enough money to put a minimal down payment on a house. Fortunately, we found a small one we could just barely afford. We were happy, but we were paying the bank 16% interest on our mortgage.

It was all quite romantic at the very beginning, until we began to realize what we had gotten ourselves into. The company's debt ramped up fast, in part due to what we owed our father. This situation was totally different than anything we three had encountered before. We were risking it all with everything being leveraged against the company, including our home mortgage. And all our savings had gone into that down payment. There was no turning back. We pushed on, knowing that the most we had in the bank at any one time was about $300. We were risking it all on the company. If Aqua-Guard didn't make it, we'd lose everything.

Aqua-Guard was going to have to be our vehicle for survival. We had to make it work. And we didn't have a safety rope to catch us if we fell. The startup's honeymoon was over within two weeks.

Little did we know we would be stuck on this fictitious bus for the next ten years.

When we were in startup mode, we didn't have a wealth of experience and insights to draw on to anticipate what lay ahead with a great deal of clarity. So we tuned into opportunity.

....

* Jim Collins, *Good to Great: Why Some Companies Make the Leap and Others Don't* (New York, NY: HarperCollins, 2001).

It had been two years since the Exxon Valdez disaster and the First Persian Gulf War. Stories of war in the Middle East and of Big Oil ruining our global environment had slowly disappeared from the news, replaced with other items such as The World Wide Web going mainstream for all to use. Bill Clinton defeating George H.W. Bush in the presidential elections and becoming president. Hurricane Andrew raising havoc on the Gulf Coast of the United States. Nirvana and Pearl Jam forming a new alternative rock music scene out of Seattle called grunge. Topics like these strangely seemed to bump war and environmental issues off the airways, at least until the next war or global environmental disaster was to happen.

As soon as oil spills were out of sight, they seemed to be out of mind. People moved on. They quickly forgot the devastation that had happened in Alaska and the Persian Gulf. But that didn't mean the devastation stopped. All the while, oil spills continued to happen around the world—from the jungles of Venezuela and Ecuador to the coastline of Scotland.

Shortly after the Exxon Valdez oil spill in Alaska, George Bush Sr. put forth the Oil Pollution Act of 1990 (OPA 90). This legislation meant that any facility or ship handling oil had to have both emergency response plans and a small amount of oil spill response equipment on hand. Large oil spill response bases, called Oil Spill Response Organizations (OSROs), were also being established. All oil tankers entering U.S. waters would have to have an agreement with an OSRO to respond on their behalf in the event of a spill.

OPA 90 *should* have been a boon for Aqua-Guard. But with a strong "Buy USA" policy and NAFTA not yet being in place (it didn't kick into effect until January 1st 1994), we could see it would almost be impossible for a Canadian startup to supply equipment into the United States.

We were forced to look elsewhere for business. We shifted our focus away from our southern neighbor to the contacts we had in countries where we had done business in the past, such as Taiwan, Thailand, Indonesia, Korea, Brazil, Venezuela and Malaysia. Even though working overseas was what we knew best, it was still very scary for a small North American company to look for opportunities in Central and South America, the Middle East and Asia.

Sometimes in business, you get a whack on the side of the head, sometimes a gentle nudge out of your comfort zone. Either can be a blessing in disguise. I believe this particular nudge to first build our business overseas actually helped Aqua-Guard survive for the long haul.

If NAFTA had been in place in 1992, we would have focused 100% on the United States. We would have had to ramp up to make a beeline into that market. And then we would have had to scrap it out with many U.S.-based competitors for the next decade. Going global first meant that, when we did enter the U.S. years later, we were able to do so as a partner with a strong, established company that already had a reputation and networks in that market. This "foreign first, backyard later" strategy—one not often followed by small North American startups—brought us great success for many years. Even today, I find it interesting that, when I attend gatherings in the U.S., 99% of all American small businesses only do business in their own country. Who knows what great opportunities, revenue streams and successes they have missed out on by not being nudged outside of their national comfort zone.

Revenue. We desperately needed a contract. Any contract.

We bid on every and any request that came across my desk, but we kept losing tender after tender. It quickly became very frustrating.

I would jump in the shower every morning, already worrying about the day ahead. Then I'd either bike to work or drive my old Volvo to the office with the same level of anxiety I had when I was freezing my ass off—literally—at those hot springs. I would get to the door of our office building and, before even putting my hand on the doorknob, be thinking:

> *What will the day throw at me once I pass through this door?*
> *What bee's nest awaits me?*
> *What crises will I have to deal with today?*

The questions were always the same, but what awaited me on the other side of the door was never predictable. It never seemed to end: every contract we bid on represented more and more risk we would have to assume...and the roller coaster just kept going. Eventually, I just started calling it "The Doorknob Effect". I learned to just take a deep breath, grab the doorknob and stride in as if I thrived on extreme stress.

It was as if my first telemark ski adventure was happening with our business. We persisted. We kept falling. We kept getting up. We'd look at our route a little differently each time and try again. We just kept getting up and trying, over and over and over again. Patience and persistence became the themes of our startup.

One day a Request for Quotation (RFQ) came across my desk from an oil company in Taiwan. I looked through the documents, hoping to find a real opportunity there. And then I found it: a crack in the specifications we could take advantage of. Jumping up from my desk, I ran into the back office where LP was. I laid the tender documents on his desk and opened them to the specs page.

"I think we have an opportunity with this Taiwanese RFQ. We can quote and supply something functional at a good price. A unique product that will be different from anything anyone else would offer."

He glanced at the papers, then looked up at me and said, "What are you thinking?"

"Look, they want an inflatable oil spill boom that when punctured won't sink."

"So, there are lots of guys who do this well. What could we do differently?"

"No one offers sealed flotation *along the top of the boom*. If we put a thin plank of foam along the length of the top, then even if the air chamber below is punctured, the foam will keep it afloat."

LP, ever practical, looked down at the specs and pushed back. "Yeah, but look at this. We have to get 330 meters of this stuff on each reel system. With all that foam on the top, it will be way too much to get on a reel."

"What if we use small 2 by 5 by 48-inch planks of bendable Ethafoam® sealed along the top?" I countered. We had used this foam before in other booms, but we'd never had to get so much product on a reel. LP dove back into the specs. I could tell he wasn't quite sold on the idea yet.

"True, that stuff bends. But we'd have to design and build it to fit onto the reels and the reels will have to fit into the shipping containers."

In my mind, I could already see the product loading onto the reel. I could see a punctured boom still floating in water because of its reserve buoyancy. So I confidently looked my partner in the eye and said, "Done! I'm going to put in a quote. Now how much will it cost?"

LP paused. "I dunno. You *really* think we have a chance?"

Without hesitating for a second, I responded to his doubt. "Yes, I do. This is different and it meets the requirements of the client. If we win, this will be quite a substantial contract. Let's go for it."

LP was enrolled. So we prepared a bid for an order of eight reels, going as low as we could on price and Sue putting together some decent payment terms. We sealed our offer in an envelope and called the courier company to take our hopes to Taiwan in time for the bid opening date.

We knew that we couldn't *not* get this contract. The demand for cash flow didn't allow us the option of falling once again. If we fell this time, we would lose everything.

Bid day came and went. We heard nothing. And then a few days later, an envelope arrived from the client. Sue, LP and I met to open it together. In it was a list of the five bidders. We were at the bottom.

I turned to LP, who looked as shocked and disappointed as I felt. "We lost it. How is that even possible? We did everything we could to enter a competitive bid...."

Before he could say anything, Sue jumped in. "Just wait a minute, guys." She had grabbed her calculator and was furiously punching in numbers. "Each bidder quoted in their own national currency, so it's hard to tell what is what...gimme a minute."

We waited, breathless, for her to raise her head.

She looked up at us and quietly said, "We are the low bid." Silence. Then firmly and loudly. "We are the *low* bid, you guys. The most expensive company is on the top of the list. ***We won the contract!!***"

We celebrated for all of 20 seconds.

Then we sat down to plan how we were going to finance, fabricate and deliver all these systems on time. The client wanted a 10% performance bond and would not issue a deposit. They finally agreed to issue a letter of credit to us, but it had conditions. We found out that we could take this letter of credit to our bank and borrow against it to help finance the fabrication of the product. That would secure enough funds to cover some of our manufacturing costs. The clincher was we wouldn't get paid in full until a third-party inspector appointed by our client certified that we had loaded 330 meters (about 360 yards) of inflatable barriers onto each of the eight reels and that they were ready to ship by the tight deadline we had agreed to. Without that quality and quantity certificate, we would not get paid *and* our bank would want their money back.

As if that pressure wasn't enough, our biggest challenge turned out to be a totally unexpected surprise.

Since we didn't actually make anything ourselves, we had to sub-contract all the bits and pieces out to different manufacturers. The boom was made in Seattle; the reels were manufactured to our design in Vancouver; the engines had to come from Japan and the air blowers from the United States. Our fate was in multiple hands. And so we waited.

Three days before our shipping deadline, I walked into our empty warehouse to find LP sitting with his head in his hands. "What's wrong?", I asked.

He looked up at me with despair in his eyes and said, "The boom is stuck in U.S. customs coming north...and the engines have not arrived from Japan yet."

"Can't we push these guys to release the goods and get the stuff here quickly?", I asked, ignorant that LP had already been doing everything he could along those lines. He went on, oblivious to my naive question. "That's not all. The reels aren't painted and we can't assemble them until they are." His shoulders caved in as he muttered, "We are fucked!"

The thing about having multiple people driving a business together is that, when one person is down, the others can help lift them up again. I didn't want to get caught up in LP's mood so I left him for a few minutes to think. When I walked back into the front office, Sue caught the look of concern on my face. "What's the matter?", she asked. Still pondering our predicament, I half-consciously replied, "I just spoke to LP and we're kinda screwed."

"Tell me the issues," said my ever-responsible sister. So I did. As I spoke, she created a list and, when I was finished talking, she passed it to me. "Here, Nigel. I have broken things up into priorities and duties. If we split up all the pieces, we can each focus on a part and get it done." We both took the list back to LP, had a brief huddle and divided up our responsibilities.

And then we got on the phones. Our little office soon sounded like the pit at the New York Stock Exchange. I was talking to our shipping agent and working with him to get things unstuck from customs. Sue was working with the engine supplier to trace their shipment to us from Japan. LP was working with our reel supplier to get the parts shipped to the painter and then returned so they could be assembled. Each of us fed off the energy of the others, the noise in the room getting louder and louder. After three hours, we paused to take stock of our situation. Exhausted, we all looked at each other and agreed it was late and it would be best to check in with our suppliers to get their status reports early the next morning.

The next day began with an early morning huddle. At 8:30, we started calling our respective suppliers. Each assured us that their product would start arriving at our warehouse within the next few hours.

We waited and waited. Then at noon a truck pulled up and the driver wandered into the office and nonchalantly said, "I got some engines for Aqua-Guard here...." We all jumped up as one. "Yup, that's us."

Forty minutes later, another truck pulled up. This driver was even more laid-back. "I got some plastic stuff for Aqua-Guard...." Here was our boom.

Sue and I both turned to LP. We needed to start loading the boom if we were going to make the deadline. Where are the reels? LP looked as frustrated as we felt. So he got on the phone with the supplier.

All we could hear was, "Yup, but...yup. But...yup. But...but when?" Sue and I looked at each other, wondering what could be up now. LP hung up and announced, "The truck bringing the first batch of four reels got in an accident after leaving the paint shop and went off the road. The axle broke and the truck is stuck. They have to bring another truck to unload and reload the reels to bring them here." That only accounted for four reels. Where were our other four? "Oh, and the second truck with our other four reels is running late. It's still being loaded at the factory."

Fortunately, we still had some work to do on the boom itself: we had to pull steel chain through a pocket in the bottom for ballast and then put aluminum connectors on the end of each 15-meter piece in order to connect the sections and turn them into a continuous 330-meter boom. This would take time.

Jeff Kermode, who had worked with us at our father's company and who had been with us on Sky Pilot when Rieko fell, took control. He and I had rock climbed, mountain biked and scuba dived in Indonesia together. Here was a guy who could carry off wearing a bright green wet suit and live with the nickname "Kermit". I trusted Jeff implicitly: we had been in several situations outside the office where we had held each other's lives in our hands and made it through. I knew I could count on him to get this critical work done. He got a team of our guys together and started painstakingly pulling 15 meters of galvanized steel chain through each boom section by hand. Then they inflated all the sections and left them out in the warehouse overnight to test for leaks.

More challenges were to come.

The next morning, the final four reels arrived on a flat deck truck. We had to borrow a forklift from our landlord to remove each one and place it in the warehouse. We soon realized that we had no space to load the reels because our warehouse was stuffed with boom.

As we unloaded the last reel from the truck, Jeff looked at me, his body dripping with sweat and hands torn up from pulling chain. He asked the question we should have asked ourselves earlier. "Where are we going to load these beasts?" LP popped his head up in the corner, where he had been turning a wrench. Sue looked down from where she was balancing on top of some boom sections. We were literally stuffed to the rafters.

The quiet that suddenly swept through the warehouse was as cold as a winter breeze. We all looked at each other and I knew everyone was thinking what I was.

What do we do now?

Jeff suddenly slipped out the back door into the hallway. Disappointed at his disappearance, I thought to myself, "What a time to leave!" Then just as suddenly he came back in and said, "Guys, there is an empty warehouse right across the hall from us. If we ask our landlord, maybe we can pull the boom through the hall and load the reels over there."

He indicated to the three of us to go out into the hall. We all dropped what we were doing to have a look at the empty, unlocked warehouse that could save our company. Sue took one look and said, "Give me a minute." She went straight to our landlord and brought her over to see the situation. Sue appealed on our behalf, explaining our predicament and our urgent need for space. "Sure," was the reply. "But if someone comes and wants to rent this spot, you guys have to leave." We agreed. Somewhere, someone was looking out for us in all this mess.

We moved two reels over to the empty warehouse and pulled the boom into the hall. Then we began loading the first reel. Jeff was operating the power unit which pulled the boom onto the reel. When his team tried to load 330 meters of boom on the first reel, they discovered we could only get 300 on.

He immediately came and explained the situation to me. I realized that if we couldn't get 330 meters on a reel our shipment would never pass inspection. Therefore, we would not be allowed to ship and if we didn't ship the product, we wouldn't be issued the shipping documents to take to the bank so that we could get paid. Everything had to be manufactured, packed and shipped, exactly as the client had requested, for the bank to release any funds to us. Everything hinged on us being able get the last 30 meters of boom onto a reel.

It felt to me like our entire enterprise was hanging over a precipice. We needed to invent our way back from the edge. I asked Jeff to look at other ways to get the boom on the reel. He huffed it back to the warehouse and came back later in the afternoon with an insight that made sense to me.

"This is just like working with a climbing rope," he said. "The more tension on the line, the more we can get on a spool." He suggested we pull the boom through the hallway and, in the other warehouse, we could chain a forklift to it. Pulling like heck, we could create tension on the line, thus minimizing the size of the boom spooling on the reel.

We had no option but to go for it, so I told Jeff to hook everything up. LP drove the borrowed forklift to pull the boom taut, I ran the power unit while Jeff guided the boom onto the reel. Sue made sure all the sections lined up well as they spooled on. At times, Jeff would be hanging off the boom like a cowboy at a rodeo, trying to keep it on track. He was in charge, yelling out to us, "200 meters....250...300...315...".

And then everything stopped.

The boom had sagged and gotten stuck underneath. We were only 15 meters short! We couldn't believe it. Jeff yelled, "Take it all off! Let's try again." This time we knew what had to be done in each of our roles. Jeff guided, Sue lined up, LP pulled and I ran the reel. Slowly. Jeff yelled out, "100...200...250...300...315." This time the reel kept turning fluidly, without obstruction. Finally we heard Jeff yell, "330! Woooohoo!"

Amazingly, applying climbing wisdom and teamwork had worked. It was almost 3:00 am by the time all the equipment was packed on the reels, but we were able to get in a few hours of sleep before the inspector was due to arrive in the morning.

330m air boom reel - Vancouver, Canada (1992)

With some simple ingenuity, a bit of patience and a lot of persistence, we survived that first contractual challenge and were paid. I've often thought about what we did together in that warehouse. It was like rock climbing, just in a different environment. We were in a life-and-death situation. We were mentally and physically exhausted. We kept leading the rope pitch and falling. Sometimes we just sat down right where we were, surrendering to the idea that there was no way we could make it. And when we were pushed to the brink, a brilliant and doable creative solution appeared.

That project gave us the cash we needed to keep going. When the money came in, we celebrated for the obligatory 20 seconds and then went right back to work to start looking for the next project.

We still had a long way to go.

CHAPTER 5
Reset

There is a certain freedom that comes with assuming the responsibility to create and run a business. But I find that freedom challenging. You really have to work at self-care. Unless you force yourself to take time off to reset, it's all too easy to succumb to guilt that you're not working long enough or hard enough.

Admittedly, sometimes Sue and I would push ourselves a little bit too hard. We had an understanding that, in order to keep our sanity, both of us would have access to the adventures we needed outside of Aqua-Guard. After Rieko and I were married, Sue and I would take turns going away. While one of us stayed with LP in the office, the other would do a trip.

In late 1991, Sue began training for a big climb up Mt. Logan in the Yukon, Canada's highest and largest mountain. Her strength and endurance training for this massive expedition involved cycling several laps of our local mountains (Cypress and Seymour), rope work and rock climbing with me on weekends, and hiking the famous local Grouse Grind with a full 60-pound pack on her back several times in a day, occasionally with Rieko for motivation.

In May 1992, Sue headed for Logan along with her friend Jackie and two mountain guides, Neil and Dwayne. I found out later that, while I was holding the fort back at the office, Sue went through hell on that massive and cold mountain.

After several weeks spent carrying loads expedition style up from their base to an 18,700-foot camp, the altitude and stress started to take its toll on Sue and

Jackie. Many nights, the temperature would drop below minus 30. Sue would occasionally vomit. But in the last afternoon that both women were to be in their tent before attempting the summit, Jackie started to vomit profusely. Sue had to scoop the puke and throw it outside. The next morning, Sue was still not feeling well: they were all worried she may have some cerebral edema (swelling of the brain) setting in. Since Sue was delusional and, obviously, could not carry on, Neil and Dwayne set her up in a tent and told her to stay there—alone—while they attempted to guide Jackie to the summit.

Just after the three left, a massive storm hit. Sue started to question why she was even there in the first place. Then in the middle of the night, she heard a noise outside her tent. She unzipped the fly and saw an exhausted man lying in the snow not far away. She went out in her tent booties and helped him inside. It was Trevor Peterson, the extreme skiing mogul, who had been my classmate for several years in high school. He was out on the mountain with another group and had become lost and dehydrated in the storm. Trevor muttered that he didn't want to die and that he wanted to see his wife and child again. Sue helped him warm up with some tea. He kept repeating he had to see his wife

Sue training for Mt. Logan - Whistler, Canada (1991)

and kids again and insisted on leaving, even though the storm was still raging outside. So, yet again, my sister was left alone in the storm.

A short while later, she thought she heard another strange sound. The wind was so loud it was tough to distinguish if it was a human being or if it was just the storm. Then she heard it again. She unzipped the tent fly and looked out into the snow-lashed blackness with her head lamp. Scanning around the tent with the beam of her light, she caught something about 20 yards away. She dragged herself out into the storm one more time and found another man, alone and exhausted, slumped over in the snow and struggling to stand up against the wind. This time it was Neil. He had spent 36 hours in pursuit of the summit. Sue helped him back into the tent.

Neil was adamant. "We have to leave. We are going to die if we stay up here!" So after warming up with some hot tea, the two struggled to pack up the tent and then headed down the mountain. After several hours of battling the weather, the storm finally broke and they were able to find their way back to the base camp, where Jackie and Neil were waiting. The two women hugged each other on sight, Jackie beaming at Sue with a gaping grin. Sue asked, "What the heck happened?" Jackie explained. "I ran out of food high on the mountain and when I got down to this camp, I found a marker for a food cache left by a previous expedition that had bailed out due to a storm. I dug down in the snow to find only deep frozen chocolate Easter bunnies. I was so hungry I took a big bite of one and broke off my front tooth."

When Sue arrived back in the office several days later, many pounds lighter and looking very drawn, I said, "Wow, it must have been a tough climb!" She looked at me and simply said, "You have no idea." She later confessed that Logan was the most difficult thing she had ever done.

I knew it was time for me to get back outdoors. Just two months before Sue's departure for her epic climb of Logan, I had had a skiing accident and snapped the ACL and MCL ligaments in my right knee. After two surgeries and six months of rigorous physical therapy, I needed to clear my head from the business, reset once again and test my knee. With Sue back from her epic climb, she and LP could hold the reins for a few weeks while I regenerated.

I had become addicted to travel and adventure, but I also had a lot of guilt around spending time and the little money we had doing what I loved to do. And I truly loved the outdoors. At the same time, I was very aware that we all had to work ridiculous hours to keep our small startup company alive.

At the time, Rieko was working crazy hours for little pay for a local travel company that arranged tours for Japanese tourists to Vancouver, Whistler and Banff. One of the perks of her job was access to super-low airfares. I will always be grateful to her for that perk, because it allowed us to go anywhere we wanted to on the planet at a time in our lives when we didn't have much money. For this particular trip, we decided to book ultra-cheap tickets to Nepal.

We landed in Katmandu, deplaned and found our bags dropped on a heap on the tarmac. We moved inside the landing hall, where we were directed to join the line to have our bags scanned. A guard was flicking his Bic® lighter inside the security scanner: obviously, the x-ray machine was broken. We waited for some time for him to identify the problem until finally, in frustration, he told us all to pass without an inspection. Outside once again, the smell of raw sewage hit my senses, just like back in Egypt several years before. We were definitely no longer at home. We pushed our way through the waiting crowd to look for Damshi, our head Sherpa and trekking guide. There he was, holding a sign saying, "AMADABLAM", the name of his trekking company.

This was another true adventure: Nepal was an amazing country with amazing people. For the next three weeks, we and five other trekkers explored the newly opened area of Annapurna South, following our 16 Sherpas on what we

Rieko & I - Nepal (1993)

found out were mostly yak tracks. We slept in British-style old canvas tents. Reminiscent of my days in Egypt, we ate fresh chicken most nights, courtesy of our Sherpas. Every day, the large bamboo baskets full of squawking live chickens that they carried got lighter.

Our new Aussie friend, Kerri, and I became super sick at the beginning of our three-week trek. For several days, we both had a very hard time keeping up with the rest of the team. Although my knee was feeling strong, my stomach was a mess. But we had no choice but to see it through. Trekking for nine to ten hours a day high in the Himalayas is challenging enough for a healthy person, never mind two sick ones. I spent most evenings in the small latrine tent (a tent covering a hole in the ground where you shit). Every morning, my quads were painfully sore from squatting over a hole for hours in the dark the night before.

Arriving in Katmandu in the early '90s was like traveling back 150 years in time: there was no infrastructure to speak of, mostly a network of dirt streets dotted with vendor stalls along the sides, many hung with meat covered in flies. But it was good to get back to even just this bit of civilization for a brief rest before our long journey back to Vancouver.

We left Katmandu to return home via Singapore and Seoul, Korea. Rieko didn't succumb to any sickness until we got on the first plane. From that moment on, she spent each connecting flight vomiting in the rear bathroom of whatever aircraft we were on. But she never complained: she has always been a real trooper. That trip home seemed to take days. We both arrived back in Canada at least 15 pounds lighter than when we had left.

As I looked out the plane's window at Vancouver's approaching lights, the knot in my stomach reappeared. I knew that the next morning would find me standing outside our office with my hand on the doorknob, wondering what the day would have in store. The guilt at having taken time off was already pulling at my soul. I believed that our company couldn't survive for a minute if I was not fully engaged 24 hours a day, 7 days a week, 365 days of the year. Things would still be in survival mode. I'd have to drop back into doing 18 to 20-hour days and working like a dog on weekends to land projects and get product out the door just to survive.

That is what I thought my life had to be like: work very hard, play very hard and travel as much as we could on Rieko's cheap airline tickets. Leave the office under a cloud of guilt and return to the same.

But something began to shift when I came back from Nepal. When I arrived in the office, I noticed that everything was still running and the company was still there. I had believed the entrepreneur's myth that we have to be shackled to our creations 24/7/365. I was mistaken. The company had survived without me.

I began to doubt another of my unconscious beliefs about being in business for yourself. The idea that it is cool to be burning the candle at both ends, getting up early and going to bed late to get everything done day after day after day. It isn't. We all need our breaks. We need to get our heads out of the fire. We need to take time away to think of the big picture. And, as I was soon to find out, we need time to take care of not only our business and ourselves, but also our family.

October 25th 1994 was the most wondrous day of my life. On that day, Rieko gave birth to our first son, Dylan. October 6th 1996 was an equally wondrous day. Our second son Devon was born. Jump ahead a few years: March 24th 2000 was the third equally wondrous day. Our beautiful daughter Kina came into the world.

Little did Rieko and I know in those early years that our end goal would be to create great global citizens.

Having young children amplified how tough life had become trying to run a business. Adding a family increased that challenge by a factor of 10. Although the joy the kids brought to us was incomparable and un-compromisable, having a family to support reinforced my awareness that we were still in survival mode. For the first two years of our sons' lives, I was traveling overseas more and more. I would be gone for six weeks at a time, starting out in Japan, then moving on to Korea, Thailand, Malaysia, Indonesia, the Philippines and Australia, then back via Singapore, Hong Kong and Taiwan. Then finally home to Vancouver. The travel was exhausting me. At one point, I even collapsed in a washroom in Taiwan and had a seizure. But what was killing me more than the exhaustion was not being there for Rieko and the family.

I felt like a gerbil on a treadmill, constantly running around putting out daily fires, always thinking about how scarce money was, and feeling like we were never really getting any further ahead.

The bigger game changer for us would be the American market. Fortunately, on January 1st 1994, the North American Free Trade Agreement had come into effect, opening the door for us to do business in Mexico and the U.S.

On a cold afternoon that same month, LP called me into the warehouse to take a peek at an oil recovery test. What I saw in front of me didn't look like much at first glance. He had rigged up a rotating hand crank with a brush on the end of it. The brush was scooping oil out of a large Tupperware bucket filled with water. As he cranked, the oil would stick to the brush and remove it from the surface. This simple technology actually worked. The brush worked like a small paddle wheel drawing surface oil towards the brush. Once the oil came in contact with the brush, it would stick.

As LP turned the crank, the brush turned. With each turn of the brush, more and more oil stuck to the brush until the bucket was clean of oil.

This wasn't even a prototype, but I could see potential in LP's crude oil skimmer. All we would have to do is scrape the oil off the brush.

I looked at him and said, "I can sell this. Build a frame, fix up a scraper to clean the brush, and put a motor in it."

I knew there was a large oil spill response trade show coming up in Seattle within the month and that Larry, the head of product sales at FOSS Environmental based in Seattle, Washington, would be there. For two years, I had been trying to build a relationship with him. He and his company had originally been heavily involved in the Exxon Valdez oil spill cleanup in Prince William Sound in Alaska. Larry had become a big player in oil spill response product sales, due to his ability to close many large equipment deals during the Valdez spill. FOSS eventually grew to become recognized as quite a big player in the industry. I had been calling Larry regularly and he kept giving me the cold shoulder. But I was determined to show him this new oil skimming system.

I begged LP to build something—anything—so I could take it with me to Seattle. LP said, "Impossible. We don't have enough time. But I'll do what I can...."

A week passed. I was sitting in the front office, afraid we were going to miss our golden opportunity, when I heard LP yell at me from the warehouse.

"Nigel, come here and see this!"

I walked through the office door into the cold. Sitting on top of an old oil drum was a gray, bare metal contraption with two white brushes mounted inside.

As I strolled over to LP, I asked, "What is that thing?"

He replied, "A prototype with a double brush and a scraping system to remove the oil from the brushes." Looking me straight in the eye, he continued, "Are you ready?" Before I could answer, he hit a switch, a small electric motor sprang into life, and the two brushes started to rotate through the scraping system. It was brilliant!

I looked at him and said, "*This is awesome!* Now can you paint it red?" LP looked at me like I was nuts, then said, "Sure."

Together, we both drove to Seattle the day before the trade show with the prototype in the trunk of my old 1980 Volvo. When we arrived at the arena, the hubbub was overwhelming. There were forklifts buzzing around, rolls of carpet being delivered, exhibit materials and people everywhere. Our small exhibit space was a 10'x10' booth with a blue curtain in the back, a small 6'x2' table and two chairs and one electric plug. We put a small tank on the table, filled it with water and placed our bright red machine inside, floating on the surface. With that, we were done setting up for the show in the morning. I did a quick tour of the arena to find out where the FOSS booth was before we left.

The next morning, we arrived early to make sure everything was working. As soon as everything checked out, I asked LP to man the booth so I could go and find Larry. Floating on air, I strutted down the aisles of the trade show floor only to find Larry surrounded by people trying to get his attention.

> *There is no way I am going to be able to get near him. This trip is going to be a wash-out unless I can get him away from his booth.*

I swallowed my discouragement and headed back to our booth. LP took one look at me and asked, "What's up? You look as if you've seen a ghost."

I told him we had to come up with a way to get Larry over to our booth. Perhaps if we caused a lot of excitement around our booth, Larry might hear about it and come on by. So we started showing our machine to everyone and anyone who walked by. Many would look at it and say, "Hey, what is that—a big boot cleaner?" or "I need one of those to clean the bottom of my boat...". Then they would chuckle and walk away. Over and over, we heard the same jokes. We were starting to lose our enthusiasm when over walked a guy with a green FOSS golf shirt on and a skippers hat.

His exhibitors' name tag said: "Joe Smith". I recognized the name: this was Larry's right hand man. Joe seemed to be heading right past our booth so I stepped out into the aisle and said, "Hi, Joe." He had that look of confusion on his face that said, "Do I know you?"

"Nigel Bennett. Aqua-Guard Spill Response, Vancouver. Nice to finally meet you."

"Oh, yeah." He relaxed into stopping for a brief conversation. "We have spoken on the phone, right?" I said, "Yup, a few times." He looked over at our booth and asked politely, "Got anything new?"

"Yes, come and take a look."

Taking a quick glance at his watch, he replied, "I have a meeting in 3 minutes."

I promised him, "This will only take one." He gingerly agreed and stepped into our booth. I introduced him to LP and asked LP to turn on the skimmer that was floating in the tank. LP hit the switch. Nothing happened. Joe said, "I gotta go."

But then the skimmer brushes started turning and picking up the vegetable oil we had added to the water that morning.

Joe looked down at the floor and then up again at me. He said, "We can sell a ton of these. I just need to show Larry."

What? Are you kidding me? Larry?

Before I could speak, Joe left and headed straight back toward the FOSS booth. In shock, I followed him. He pushed his way through the crowd to Larry and whispered something into his ear. Larry turned and pushed his way back through the crowd with Joe leading the way. I rushed back to our booth before they arrived. I whispered in LP's ear, "Shit, here they come. All or nothing now...."

Larry arrived and grunted at us in his deep voice, "Let's see how this thing works."

LP hit the switch again and the brushes started to turn. Larry looked on with a poker face and didn't say anything. He turned to Joe and whispered something. They both nodded, then turned and, without saying a word to us, walked away.

I thought, "What? They came over and...nothing? Who do they think they are?"

We were pretty disappointed. We thought we had them sold. Silently, we packed up after the show and put the demo unit back in the trunk of the car. There wasn't anything to say.

On our way north to the Canadian border, my old Motorola cell phone rang. Both Larry and Joe were on the crackling line.

Larry spoke first, "You guys might have something there. We are quite interested in distributing this for you. Do you have any distributors?"

LP was driving and looked over at me. I said to Larry, "Not on the west coast." LP glanced across at me like I was crazy. We actually didn't have a distributor anywhere in the United States. I told them we were interested in a deal and would consider giving FOSS Alaska, Washington and Oregon as a test.

Larry replied, "Sounds good for now...but the price has to be right."

We agreed to draft some things up when we arrived back in our Vancouver office.

I hung up, looked over at LP and yelled, "We fucking got them!"

Now that we had a distributor for our crude prototype of an oil skimmer for three states, we had to dig in. LP created in the back warehouse and I marketed the shit out of this new oil skimmer from the front office. Within a few months, we had a fully tested production model. All we needed were clients.

A few months later, Larry called me with another opportunity. "Nigel, Alyeska Pipeline Service Company is looking to upgrade their oil spill response capabilities for the Valdez Marine Terminal. They need skimmers for every pump station along the pipeline. They may need 30+ machines. Can you guys give me a good price quote for 30+ machines with all the bells and whistles?"

I agreed and walked in the back to talk to LP about pricing. While I was writing up the numbers we came up with, Larry called back. "Not sure if this is going to work as Alyeska needs some pretty specific equipment and they must be able to manhandle each machine through the bush if necessary. Many of the pump stations are near river crossings in very remote areas. I don't think your machines are a fit: they are too heavy and not that portable."

I stopped Larry before he could go further. "Wait. Give us a chance. What exactly do they need?"

Larry said, "Each system will have to be able to be broken down and carried into the wilderness by two people. That's their requirement."

"I am sure we can do this. Give us a few hours to get back to you," I offered.

Larry agreed, "...but we can only wait a couple of hours."

I walked back to talk to LP again. I firmly believed in his ability to come up with a solution at the eleventh hour. After I explained the situation, he looked at me yet again and said, "You told me if we could design this technology, you could sell it."

"That's true," I admitted. "But this is a huge opportunity for us. All we have to do is break the parts down so two guys can huff them through the bush."

LP replied, "Easy for you to say." He thought for a moment and then agreed to give it a go.

"Great. You have two hours to come up with a solution."

Ninety minutes later, LP called me into his office and showed me a drawing board with a bit of drafting paper stuck to it. He had sketched out each piece of the equipment: the oil skimmer head, the diesel/hydraulic power pack, the pump and the hose package. The genius of his design was that each piece could be lifted onto two stretcher carry poles. The hoses would all be stored in a bag that also could be carried by these poles.

Our two hours were up.

I called Larry back and told him we could do it and would have a quote and specification sheet to him by the end of the day. On that basis, Larry agreed to put forth our proposal to the client.

Days went by. Finally Larry called. "I have good news. We have an order for 33 systems. I will get you a purchase order shortly."

Trying to hold back my excitement, I calmly replied, "OK, Larry. Thanks very much. I look forward to seeing it and getting to work on this order for you."

I hung up the phone. Sue was sitting across from me and could see that I had started shaking. She leaned over and asked me, "We got it?" All I could mutter was, "Yup." I stood up and walked out into the warehouse and yelled.

"Woooohoo! We did it. We got the order!"

LP looked up from his work and quietly said, "The Alyeska one?"

I said "yup" again. He looked at me with real concern in his eyes and said, "Oh shit! When do we have to deliver?"

Every entrepreneur dreams of hitting the mother lode. But when you actually land that first big client or that first big order, you have to be quick on your feet to make it happen on time.

From then on, Larry and Joe from FOSS were able to sell our two-man systems all over the west coast. They even equipped their own oil spill response bases all over the U.S. and overseas with them. For the next year or so, we were busy filling orders, sorting out manufacturing and shipping delays. We now started to experience the challenges of fast growth: trying to fill as many orders on time without sufficient infrastructure in place to scale up operations.

Our persistence was starting to pay off. But we still had to keep our noses to the grindstone. Who had time to look up from all the orders we were filling?

We were still a tight team. But we were stuck running. It seemed we were always running. And the faster we ran, the faster the years seemed to fly by. I couldn't keep up this pace. I needed change. But in my mind, I was just too busy to look outside my "shire" for help.

CHAPTER 6
Help!

Times were not easy.

By late 1996, the Bennett home was filled to the brim. Rieko had quit her job in the travel industry and was now running a daycare from our basement. Our boys were doubled up in their bedroom. All empty spaces in the house had to bring in money. We rented out the garage and part of our small driveway to a neighbor with a boat. We had international students living with us and a tenant in the basement. All just to make ends meet.

I was still traveling a lot. So Rieko would drive our boys to pre-school each morning in her father's old Nissan. The floorboards were so rusted that the boys would giggle about seeing the road underneath them through the holes. We were in full survival mode and didn't even know this had become our "normal". The rusted out car floor was just symbolic of our life: even though it was dangerous to drive, we thought we couldn't afford to fix it.

Back at Aqua-Guard, we three bus drivers were learning on the fly. None of us had received any formal business training. I was so focused on our day-to-day survival that I didn't have time to look up from the current crisis of the moment to seek any outside help. But that was about to end.

Help was going to find me.

Trevor, a professional football player who was a good friend of Dave and who was also becoming a buddy of mine, called me up and insisted I go with him to check out a group called "The Young Entrepreneurs' Organization" (YEO). Trevor really wanted me to join this group. He kept going on and on about how it had really been helping him in his recent transition from professional sports to business. How it was helping him focus on the balance between his business and family life. Joining, he said, had helped him get his head out of his ass.

The little voice in my head said (yet again):

> *"Nigel, you don't have time for something like this. You are just too busy."*

I also really didn't want to hang around with a bunch of pompous perceived millionaires: that just wasn't my scene. I preferred hanging out in the mountains or in the backcountry on skis.

A few days later, Trev called me again and insisted I come on a recruitment boat cruise. I tried to get out of it and used every excuse in the book. But this was Trevor inviting me. He had been a 300-pound lineman. When he insisted on something, people tended to do it. So I eventually said, "Sure, I'll go."

We boarded a massive private yacht, teeming with waiters weaving their way through a crowd of about 90 people with trays of wine and small appetizers. Everyone was dressed to impress.

> *Oh god, what is this? What have I gotten myself into?*

It was too late for me to get off the boat. We had already left the dock.

Before I could find a quiet corner to myself, a fellow wearing a dark suit strode through the crowd towards me. Putting out his hand, he said, "Hi, I'm Lance Bracken." His powerful grip, intense gaze and relaxed presence put my suspicions to rest and we ended up chatting together for about 40 minutes. Lance candidly shared with me his struggles in managing a hyper fast-growing company while raising a young family. He told me how YEO had helped him feel that he was not alone. He had joined a YEO Forum group called "No Limits", a small gathering of like-minded business owners (called "entrepreneurs"—I couldn't even pronounce this word at the time!), most with young families, who were all trying to make a go of it.

I leaned in with interest to hear more over the loud chatter around us. Lance confessed, "Before joining, I felt totally alone. I had no one to share the experiences I was going through with. The guys in my forum group changed all that."

Call it serendipity or luck, but this was exactly what I had been looking for. I had been inadvertently searching for this kind of peer support for several years and didn't even know it existed.

Then it struck me. Bingo!

> *There actually are other people in the world like me. Young entrepreneurs trying to get a business off the ground AND have a life!*

From that point on, we chatted away as if there was no one else on the boat. Later, Lance introduced me to some of the members in his "No Limits" group. I realized that we were all literally and metaphorically in the same boat. We all had our heads down with our young businesses, not knowing which way to turn, just dealing with each day as it came at us. Most had young families.

What surprised me most of all was that these guys didn't seem to be the stuck-up, rich playboys I had envisioned them to be. They were regular guys like me, young businessmen giving everything to getting their small companies off the ground while they tried to raise a family at the same time.

That conversation with Lance was an extremely significant turning point for me. Shortly after meeting him, I became a member of his forum. Over time, I became extremely close to all the guys in our "No Limits" group. The decision to connect myself with the Young Entrepreneurs' Organization would end up changing my life, Rieko's life and our children's lives forever.

Over the next 15 years, the guys in my forum group all became like brothers. The uniqueness of our group was because of the people, not the YEO organization per se. We had a very strict constitution that every member had to sign: we had to attend monthly meetings, pay penalties for being tardy or missing, and keep everything that was shared in strict confidence. There was to be no finger pointing, no statements like "You need to do this...". Just sharing from experience—and those experiences had to be our own. We also held two retreats a year in which each member would get a chance to present personal or business items of importance in their life to the group. The group members would then share their experiences with the same or a similar issue or situation. Many times, we would bring in an outside facilitator to help us follow our strict protocol of "no advice—just sharing".

In all of this, it was up to each of us to find value in the shared experiences and in the safe space of confidentiality. I certainly did.

My experience up to then had been that our Aqua-Guard business was so unique that no one on the outside could possibly understand what I was going through. With this input from Lance and the "No Limits" group, my thinking quickly began to shift. I thought I was a tough nut to crack, but their conversations opened me up. Each of our monthly meetings filled me with so much sharing and learning about the family/business balance. I came to understand that all businesses are similar, and that all business owners have a lot to share. Most of the time, we feel isolated, incorrectly believing that no one can possibly understand what we deal with on a day-to-day basis. Yet isolation can be one of the biggest things blocking us from learning what we need to know.

What do I mean by that? Well, I noticed that, for the first few years, pretty much everyone in our forum group, including me, operated in survival mode. But as we shared our failures and what we did wrong but would not repeat, as we shared the stories of what we did to get through it all and celebrated each other's victories, things started to change for the better. At times, tears were shed. We became tight brothers who could trust each other. With this trust came results. We helped one another with tough business decisions and difficult personal issues. When we opened up to the group, magic happened. And, in time, we all started moving in a positive direction. And then things started to speed up.

By 1999, Dave Ash was becoming a bit of the hero in our YEO forum group. He had a very successful fast-growing company, but what intrigued me the most about him was his heavy involvement in giving back to Vancouver's downtown East Side community. One of the city's oldest and poorest neighborhoods, the East Side had fallen from being the political, cultural and retail center of Vancouver to being the center of prostitution, open-air drug trafficking and homelessness.

About a week before we were scheduled to fly to San Diego for a YEO learning event, Dave introduced us all to "Street Mom". Dave had asked her to attend our monthly meeting as a speaker. This 60-year-old lady rode around town on an electric-powered wheelchair with one soul purpose in life: to help the homeless kids and youth living on the streets of Vancouver. She shared her story with us. Every morning, she prepared sandwiches and other easy-to-carry, nutritious food in her small East Side apartment. Every day, without fail, she would drive around in her scooter to meet kids in the back alleyways and lanes to feed them. She did this, day after day, as a volunteer. Her goal was to keep the kids away from the predators. I was overwhelmed by what she was able to accomplish. Even with her disability, she was able to give so much of herself to the youth in need in our city.

The image of Street Mom purposefully driving through the streets stayed with me as I made my way to San Diego. The plan for this YEO event was to learn as much as I could from the 500 other members attending from all over the world. Yet what I remember most from that trip, and what I will never forget, are a few moments of a conversation I had with Dave sitting at the end of a lunch table on the Coronado Hotel's patio.

I looked quizzically at him and asked awkwardly, "How do you know?"

"Know what?" was his quick comeback.

I began again. "How do you know where to help? How do you choose where you want to help in the world? I know I want to do something...but I don't know where to start. And how do you do so much?"

Dave gently replied with calm confidence. "Nigel, don't overthink it. Just take your first step. Just give. It might be to a homeless man on the street: give him five bucks. Don't ask questions, just go with it. Or perhaps you might give of yourself. So your first step might be volunteering in a soup kitchen. Just call them up and ask how you can help. Once you do your first thing, then the second will appear. It will all make sense. Don't force it. Let it happen. You will see."

> *I have no idea what the heck Dave is talking about. He's doing so much...how and where should I start?*

When we landed back in Vancouver several days later, my head was still buzzing with Dave's words. As I exited the airport on the "Park&Fly" mini-bus, it was dark and pouring with rain. I picked up my car from the long-term parking lot and began the 45-minute drive home. As I was heading up Boundary Road, a homeless man with wet tattered clothes was standing on the meridian. His smudged cardboard sign read, "Her lawyer was better than mine, please help." The light turned red just as I reached the intersection, so I stopped and began rummaging through my wallet to find some bills. When I rolled down my window, the burst of cold wind and rain on my face felt like a slap. I waved to the man to come over to my car, and I handed him some cash. He looked at me with a smile and said, "Thank you, sir." Then he turned and walked through the large curbside puddle to the next car behind me.

As the light changed to green and my car started to move on up the road, an inexplicably strong feeling came over me.

Dave's chat with me in San Diego echoed in my head. All I had done was give a stranger a few dollars on a stormy night. But this time, when I gave, it was as if my soul was on fire. What I had just done didn't seem enough. I was filled with this amazing energy, a sense of wonder and a new question.

What might be possible if I gave more than just my money?

I could start giving of myself, rather than just signing a cheque each year to various charities to make me feel better about myself. I could start getting involved and offering my time and energy.

The next week, I told my sons Dylan and Devon, who were then five and three years old, about "Street Mom". Devon looked up at me and asked, "Can we get her some money?" Dylan enthusiastically answered, "Let's have a garage sale and give all the money to Street Mom." So we rounded up all our stuff that we didn't really need and had a huge garage sale. Street Mom could use some well-deserved publicity, so we called our local newspaper and they came and interviewed the boys and took a photo. The next day we arranged to meet Street Mom on her rounds to give her a $700 cheque for the money the boys had raised. She was struck that two little guys could raise so much for her with a simple garage sale. And I was struck when I saw that my boys had this "soul on fire" light in their eyes, too, as they chatted with her.

What might be possible if I gave more of myself?

It's amazing how one small, conscious question can lead you to a whole new outlook on life. Little did I know this was going to be the first of many insightful questions that would ultimately guide me towards getting unstuck and evolving into the entrepreneur, family man, philanthropist and human being I am today.

I wasn't the only one at Aqua-Guard beginning to question things. Sue and I had been working together now for almost a decade. But events outside of work were having her wonder whether a future with Aqua-Guard was what she really wanted.

Sue had been good friends with Jim Haberl, a professional guide with Whistler Heli-Skiing, since forever. Jim, who was actually quite famous in the climbing community, was also her mentor. Back in 1993, he and his lifelong buddy Dan

Culver had been the first two Canadians to summit Pakistan's treacherous mountain K2 in the Himalayas. After celebrating on the summit for only a few minutes, the two began their descent. On their way down, Dan fell to his death. His body was never found. Jim was never really the same after that.

Early in their friendship, Jim and Sue had climbed a route up the famous Stawamus Chief in Squamish, British Columbia called "The Split Pillar". The Chief is a giant granite rock face similar to El Capitan in Yosemite. I still remember rushing out of our North Vancouver office with my camera late one afternoon. After a fast 45-minute drive from our office, I arrived in Squamish at the base of the Chief to catch some photos of their attempt. There they were, about a thousand feet up, barely visible from the ground through my telephoto lens and obviously hunkered down for the night in their portaledges high off the valley floor. The next day they would summit, which ended up being quite an accomplishment for my little sister at the time.

Sue & Jim - The Chief, Canada (c1998)

On April 29th 1999, Sue got a call at the office that her friend Jim had died that day in an avalanche in Alaska. He was 41.

Jim had been attempting a first ascent of a remote, unnamed peak in Wrangell-St. Elias National Park with mutual friends Keith Reid and Graeme Taylor. The three had stopped for a break high up on the mountain in an exposed spot. It was too dangerous to rope up. So Jim had decided to do a re-con. As he began to climb a few yards up to get a better view of their route, the snowpack started to move. When the slow-moving slab stopped, Keith and Graeme were visible, but they couldn't find Jim. He had been swept over a massive cliff. When they climbed down the mountain, they found his body a thousand feet below. According to the *Whistler Pique News* the next day, "A spokesman for the Alaska State troopers said the three were not in a dangerous situation, just in the wrong place at the wrong time."

Jim had written two books about his climbing adventures. The first, *K2: Dreams and Reality*, which he had self-published in 1994, had been followed by *Risking Adventure*, published by Raincoast Books. This later collection of five stories of climbs and expeditions from around the world had one overarching theme: follow the passion of your heart, trust that—go with the feeling.

Both Jim's wife and my sister heeded those words. They decided they wanted to visit the area where he had died. So a month later, Keith agreed to lead them back to that unnamed peak in Alaska.

The trip was really tough for all of them—and not just emotionally. They flew into the area in a small plane called a CUB. Keith flew in first and landed on a glacier with their supplies. The women came out later that day in a second flight. As they approached the glacier, Keith signaled them to throw out their plastic sleds with their gear to lighten the load for a better landing. But when the women threw one of the plastic gear sleds out, it got hung up on the rear flap of the plane.

The pilot looked back and yelled out to them. "Fuck—we are going down!" They hit the glacier hard and bounced a few times before they came to rest. Fortunately, everyone was OK. But the plane was damaged. So they unloaded the rest of the gear, and then Keith helped the pilot repair what they could. After a while, the pilot muttered, "Let's see if this works." They aligned the plane with the length of the cracked glacier and prepared for takeoff. Heading down slope, the plane built up enough speed to rise into the air. If the pilot made it back to base safely, he would return to pick them up in a few days. During that time, the three adventurers skied into the location where Jim's body had been found, towing their gear on sleds. They achieved a bit more closure by doing a little ceremony in honor of Jim there. And then they returned to the rendezvous point on the glacier where the pilot picked them up as scheduled.

The stress of Jim's death, this trip and other issues took their toll on Sue. In December of 2000, she decided she had had enough. She came to me and asked if she could be bought out of Aqua-Guard. She was intent on divorcing her husband, selling her condo and moving to a ranch that was for sale in the interior of the province. She really wanted to create a very different lifestyle, trading in her climbing ropes and crampons for horses and cattle.

When we sat down to discuss it, I could tell this was where her passion was leading her. Together, we came up with a vendor-financed deal that would buy her out over four years and leave me as majority shareholder. Over the next few years, she would get married again (this time to a wrangler) and adopt two girls.

It was tough to see her go. Not only because she was my sister. But her talent at keeping LP and I in check and at managing our finances was going to be very hard to replace. Fortunately, we were able to poach our competitor's general manager to keep things above water.

I quickly realized that having a founder as a partner, someone with skin in the game, is quite different from hiring a manager who clocks in each morning and clocks out each night and has no skin in the game. Salaried employees didn't engage with the same level of passion that we founders did. They didn't assume the same level of risk each day that we founders had. And they slept well at night. Over the next while, this difference in mindset became quite difficult for LP and I. Passionate engagement would be virtually impossible to duplicate unless we created things in such a way that our GM had major skin in our game.

CHAPTER 7
A Shift

There's a whole different level of determination and persistence available when you have everything on the line. I knew exactly what that felt like, thanks to Sue's boyfriend Ken, and an adventure he and I had had in Squamish, British Columbia back in the fall of 1987.

Ken was like a mountain goat of a climber, strong and a generally great mountain man. Like a mentor, he was always pushing me to get better, to do things I didn't think I could possibly do. This time out, he agreed that, if I would "clean" the climb, he would lead the most difficult sections of a 12-pitch route called the Buttress Connection that we had chosen to take up the face of the infamous 2,300-foot Stawamus Chief. I was actually terrified of rock climbing, even though Sue and I lived to climb in those days. Never the strongest climber in any of our groups, I would always let someone else lead. I agreed to "clean" for Ken, knowing that the higher up we went, the more exposed we would be and the more I'd want an experienced champ like him leading.

It was still dark the morning we hiked into the base of the Chief. Looking up at the route we had planned from the base of the cliff was quite daunting. "Diedre", as it was called, was a beautiful crack that ran all the way to the top of the Chief's apron. We both checked all our gear: we each had a rack of protective equipment slung from our shoulders, harnesses with bags filled with chalk for our hands, rock climbing shoes, a small water bottle and a 50-meter rope (approximately 160 feet).

Ken agreed to lead the first segment. He easily moved up this first "pitch", or part of the climb equal to one rope length, and set up a belay station to bring me up. He yelled down to me, "On belay!" This meant he had me safely roped into the station and I could start climbing. As lead climber, he had placed pieces of protection (an expanding cam device) into the crack every ten to fifteen feet and then clipped the rope into each "piece" via a carabineer. As "cleaner", I would move up behind him to the next piece above me, un-clip the carabineer, remove the piece from the crack and then re-clip the piece and carabineer onto my rack of protection. Our plan was to repeat this same maneuver all the way up the 12 pitches.

I had climbed Diedre many times in the past and felt comfortable leading the lower pitches. So I agreed to lead the second one. There are three scary things about climbing this way. First, you are relying on a rope and a few pieces of protection, tiny little expanding devices wedged in a crack, to hold you if you fall. Not a bolt or a piton securely pounded into hard rock. Second, as leader, the farther away you are from the last piece of protection, the farther you have to fall. So if I am leading ten feet out and I slip, I'll fall 20 feet before my rope will catch me. And third, we could only carry so much weight, so we were packing a finite number of pieces. Using them sparingly but safely was an art.

We knew our hands and feet would take a beating this day. Being the lead in a crack climb can be tricky—and painful. As I passed Ken's last piece, I would stuff my hand inside the crack ahead of me (if the crack was large enough) and then expand my fist in order to pull myself up. Skin would peel off my knuckles and my hands would bleed. Or if the crack was too small, I would use my fingers to grab hold of any crystal of granite outside the crack that would hold me. The sharp edges of the granite would tear my fingertips.

As for my feet, well, let's say rock climbing shoes have to fit tightly and so they are probably one of the most uncomfortable types of shoes ever made. The soles of the pair I was wearing that day were made of what we call 5.10 rubber, which meant they would literally stick to almost anything. And that was good. Because on today's climb we would have to stuff our feet into cracks sideways and then twist our feet to jam them in securely enough so we could stand on them. Momentary relief for our hands, arms, legs and, most of all, our feet would only come when we paused at a belay station.

For the first few hours, we took turns at leading up the pitches, inching our way up the solid granite wall high above the little town of Squamish and beautiful Howe Sound. As we moved higher and higher, we knew that the crux pitch was still to come. I think Ken could tell by the quiver in my voice that the exposure was starting to get to me like it had before on Sky Pilot. But he kept pushing me to go beyond what I thought my limits were. I actually did feel stronger and stronger after each pitch, even though we were getting higher and higher on the rock face.

We finally made it to one of the last sections of the climb: the crux 5.10c pitch, which was quite difficult and very exposed. I was clipped into a belay station on a ledge below Ken. He carefully started up the pitch, secured a few pieces, and then began looking for a place to insert the next one into the crack.

Suddenly Ken was doing a ten-foot screamer down the rock face right above me! The rope went taut. I had him secured. He looked down at me and said, "Man, I am tired. This pitch is a bitch."

He paused for a moment before moving back up past his last piece. I could hear him grunting all the way.

> *This is rare for Ken. He's usually like a machine.*

Foooooff....down he came again. The line stretched taut again: this time it was a fifteen-foot screamer. I scraped the skin on my hands against the rock face. But, again, I had him. This time, though, he asked me to lower him down.

> *We're about 1,500 feet off the deck and mountain man Ken wants me to lower him back to the belay station?*

I must have frozen because he asked me again. When I got him down to my level, I could see that he was out of breath. He said, "I can't go on, buddy. You are going to have to finish this."

I didn't even try to hide my fear. I had been relying on Ken to lead me to the top. I looked him straight in the eye and shouted, "Are you fucking crazy! I've done quite a bit of climbing over the past few years, even climbed a few 5.10c pitches. But not at 1,500 feet off the ground—totally exposed!"

There was a long silence between us. "I don't think I can do it," I muttered.

"We have no choice," he said. "Either you go up...or we both will have to go all the way down. And we don't want to have to do that."

Reluctantly, I agreed with him. He gave me the rack of climbing pieces, looked at me confidently and said, "You're on belay!" Off I went, inching towards where he had just fallen. I worked my way up past each securing piece he had left in the rock, grunting as I climbed higher and higher up the smooth granite.

Don't look down. Look at the rock. Keep going. Focus!

I got to Ken's last piece, rested for a moment, and then moved up about eight feet past it to a nice spot in the crack we were following to where I could place an expanding cam. Now the tricky part. With both my feet smeared against the rock face, I held on to the rope with one hand. With the other, I unclipped a carabineer from my shoulder rack and placed the friend in the crack, pulled it a few times to make sure it was secure, and then clipped the rope into it.

This is totally nuts! I am way out of my league here. This is pretty much the most insane thing I have ever done in my life.

I looked down at Ken and he must have sensed my self-doubt. He yelled up, "Great work, Nige. Keep going."

I took in a deep breath of his confidence and carried on. Up and up I went, doing my best to figure out where to put pieces into the rock. My legs started shaking like a sewing machine. I was spent. But I focused and pushed on. There was no other way out of this situation: I had to make it.

Suddenly I slipped and it was my turn to go screaming down the rock face. I could hear the loud "pop" as the last piece I had placed pulled out of the stone. That slowed my fall down a bit, but not entirely. I only hoped I would come to a full stop. Suddenly my belaying harness went tight around my legs and waist and the air in my lungs expelled in a loud "Ooooommmmmff". The elasticity in the rope had broken my fall. Ken had me: I was safe.

Ken looked up and yelled, "Didn't expect that one. You OK?"

I glanced down in his general direction and grunted. I knew I had to finish this beast. I had to find the determination to go on—for the both of us.

Another breath and then I started climbing again. Each move had to be thought through. I would either jam a hand into the rock crack so I could pull my full body weight up on the edges of my fingertips. Or I would twist a foot into some crazy position to fit in the crack so I could push myself higher. I got to the piece that had popped out and replaced it. Up and up I went, now hyper-focused. Until I saw right above me a bolt-and-chain station.

Shit! A freaking hanging belay...you have got to be kidding! This is getting way too crazy....

The crack we had been following had ended. I would have to full smear up 15 feet of rock to make the belay station. That meant 15 terrifying feet of pressing the soles of my climbing shoes directly to the rock and using friction to gain vertical ground.

All my life I have been terrified of heights. I can't go higher than ten or twelve stories in a building, and elevators give me the creeps. Leading this was *way* beyond my comfort zone. This was entering my own personal no man's land. But I had to.

I yelled towards Ken, "The last bit is pretty lead out to the belay station!" Ken replied, "Yup...a heck of a screamer if you go, buddy. But I have you, don't worry!"

My hands and legs were shaking like a leaf, whether from exhaustion or fear I couldn't tell. I took yet another super deep breath, then pushed up past the last piece I had placed out onto the open granite. Trying to keep my body poised like a cat and not hug the rock too close, I mumbled to myself:

> *Keep three points on the rock at all times. Three points on the rock at all times. Three points...on...the...rock.*

I lurched forward inch by inch, higher and higher, farther and farther away from my last bit of protection. I could see the hanging chain from the belay glistening in the sun a mere eight feet above my head. At some moment, I would have to go for it. I didn't care about my technique: I just needed to reach that chain. So I threw my whole weight into a lunge, grabbed ahold of the chain and pulled myself up to the belay station.

Clipping into the steel ring that hung down from the chain, I set up a belay for Ken and yelled, "Off belay!" That signaled to him that I was safely clipped to the station. Looking down from a position of relative comfort hanging in the air, I could barely see my climbing partner at the bottom of our 50-meter rope. He yelled up to me, "Good work, buddy."

Now I just had to put Ken on belay and bring him up. It took me a while to get my shit together. Finally he was on. I shouted out, "On belay!" Ken gradually worked his way up to the station, cleaning the pieces we had both set along the way. We both laughed with relief when he arrived at my level and we could pause to take a look around us.

The view was amazing. I heard awe and a bit of worry in his voice as he said, "Oh shit, this is high."

> *No freaking kidding!!!!*

And suddenly my mind was filled with fear again and I began to shake. In spite of that, I lead the next pitch up to a ledge. On either side of the ledge was a drop straight down to the valley floor nearly 2,300 feet below. For the last while, we had been making our way up the side of a massive ravine. As I set up the next belay for Ken, I gratefully realized we'd be able to sit with our feet hanging over this ledge and rest here for a bit before we made the final push to the top.

That didn't happen until late in the day. As we came up over the top of the Chief's massive granite head with all our gear hanging off us, we were met by a group of hikers who had walked up the backside of the mountain. The looks on their faces were priceless: where had these two guys, hands bleeding, exhausted and weighted down with ropes and gear, come from? I looked over at Ken to see he was smiling. I coughed quietly and said loud enough for the hikers to hear, "Nice view, eh?"

That climb was a great metaphor for so much of what I had been experiencing in the rest of my life. Over the years, I had noticed that I often had trouble focusing on the "normal" day-to-day stuff. But if my life or someone else's life depended on me, if something really important was on the line, when the "chips were down" and there was nowhere else to go, I could focus, come up with solutions and have amazing things happen. Push me to the max, put me in a situation where I didn't know if we were going to make it and *somehow* I would push through. Every time, I'd discover things about myself I had never dreamed of.

Our whole adventure with Aqua-Guard was like an unending series of difficult pitches. Each pitch demanded our super concentration and super focused effort as business leaders. Each pitch left our hands a little more bloodied, each belay station gave us five minutes clipped into safety before we had to push on and begin moving towards the next goal and the next challenge. Some pitches had us face what we thought were our limits. Others were real screamers. And still others pushed us to create something entirely new to avoid any of the many possible ways we could fall to our deaths.

Many pitches, many deals, taken together, made up our climb from relative obscurity as a Canadian startup to international recognition as a leader in oil spill response technology.

Perhaps that's why, at one point, we decided to install a real ship's bell in our office. We would work so hard to close a deal, to complete a sale, and we knew we could only celebrate for a few seconds. That's what the big brass bell was for. Whenever someone rang it, we would come together for a huddle, do high fives all around, and share a brief summary of what had happened. And then, just as quickly, we'd disperse to either dive into all the work that came with each "win" or to keep delivering on our existing promises to clients. The more the bell in our office rang, the more persistence and stamina we had to have to keep going.

Somehow there had to be a way to move with life, a way where we didn't end up feeling as if we were being thrown from one side of a hard, brass bell to the other with each deal and each new client. I trusted that someday we'd be able to appreciate, maybe even enjoy, how we were developing as people through all this. Perhaps somewhere along the way we'd find the sweet spot where those extended periods of pushing ourselves to the limit, with our feet pressed into the rock face in an effort to fulfill our dreams, were better balanced with moments at our belay stations where we could enjoy the view, linger in the euphoria of accomplishment and share the best of ourselves with the people we cared about most.

Now that Sue had left Aqua-Guard, I sensed that sweet spot would be tougher and tougher for me to find.

Sue wasn't the only one having doubts about the future. Perhaps it was burnout. Perhaps the beginnings of a mid-life crisis. But in 2003, I found myself talking to my business coach about wanting to sell everything and have a simple life.

I was still working with Terry, the same coach who had helped us orchestrate our break-off from my father's company and whom I had been working with one-on-one for the past five years. More and more of what I talked about with Terry in our breakfast meetings dealt with my personal issues, rather than with the business or my business relationships.

Acknowledging this shift in my needs, he told me that the personal stuff was not his specialty, and suggested I reach out to Kevin Lawrence, another coach who had helped him deal with such matters and whom he thought could be a good match for me. I must have hesitated because he said, "Give him a call and feel him out. You'll know if he is a fit once you meet face to face. He may be a bit expensive, but he's worth every penny."

I was at my wit's end. So I took his suggestion. I called Kevin and we had a really good chat. We agreed to meet in person in a boardroom downtown for a full-day exploratory session. After the first thirty minutes, I said, "Look, Kevin, I just feel like leaving my company to go sell t-shirts on the beach. And, honestly, I don't do well in boardrooms. Let's walk and talk."

So we headed down to Vancouver's Seawall where I could smell the sea air and hear the squawking of seagulls as we walked around Stanley Park. I was bursting at the seams. So I dumped everything on Kevin: my history, my father's story, issues brewing with my business partner, how tough it was raising three kids. Everything. After five hours of walking, resting at benches and refueling at coffee shops, I knew he was right for me. Handing him a check, I asked him if he would be willing to be my coach. We are still together to this day. Hiring Kevin as my coach was the second most important choice I made about who I needed in my life as an entrepreneur. Thankfully, I chose wisely and both the Young Entrepreneurs' Organization and Kevin have positively impacted my business and personal life for years.

Over the next several months, Kevin and I explored all the things that were in the way of my success and happiness. We literally drew this as an "asteroid belt" of issues. The idea was that we would pick off one asteroid at a time to work on, starting with the smaller ones first. Once we got into a rhythm, we could start tackling some of the larger ones. We would deal with each issue head on, Kevin holding me accountable to face and work through each asteroid before I would move on to the next. Kevin called this "Licking the Toad": deal with the ugly stuff first so you can get it out of the way. The first were brutally difficult to deal with. But once I dealt with one, then two, each successive one became easier and easier until eventually we had enough momentum to deal with issues head on.

Great things started to happen very quickly in my life.

In 2006, I was accepted to participate in a business program associated with MIT called "The Gathering of Titans" (GOT). When I arrived in Boston, I took a taxi straight to Dedham, the satellite campus of the Massachusetts Institute of Technology. Students of the GOT program, all business owners, would stay either in an old New England mansion that had been bequeathed to the Institute or in a hotel down the road. Sessions would take place in a small 75-seat conference center on the large grounds. Locked down on site for four days, we would be maximizing the contact and networking time we had with each other.

As my taxi pulled up to the mansion, I saw a lineup of limousines and town cars filling the driveway.

> *What the heck am I doing here? This place is for smart people—not for a dyslexic guy who barely made it through college and who has virtually no business training.*

Resisting the urge to throw up, I thanked the taxi driver and stepped from the cab into the lobby. There I met my roommate, Gary from Chicago, who was also checking in. We instantly got along. Both new to this whole thing, we decided to sit beside each other in the conference room during introductions. The little voice in my head, meanwhile, kept chattering away.

> *What the heck am I doing here? What was I thinking when I agreed to come? I hated everything about my previous schooling experiences....*

And then my internal musings were drowned out by the rumbling and whispers around me. A guy in a suit had just stepped into the room and everyone was remarking, "That's Verne Harnish...". I had no idea who this Verne was or why people were so excited.

Verne took his place at the front of the room, greeted us and then threw a question out into the room.

"Who here has a coach or has been coached?"

I gingerly raised my hand, something I had never done in all my years at high school and technical college. I looked around the room and was amazed to see that there were only three of us with our hands in the air.

Verne said, "Let me tell you guys that anyone who is successful has a coach or even multiple coaches. Steve Jobs of Apple, Bill Gates of Microsoft, Michael Dell of Dell Computers, even presidents of countries have coaches. The most strategic thing you can do as a business leader and owner is to get a good coach."

I was blown away. I had thought I was the last one on the bandwagon here.

I will never forget what Verne said next. "If you are an entrepreneur, you need help. You need a coach: you need to surround yourself with people who are smarter than you. You cannot create a successful business and a successful, happy life by yourself. It is impossible to do it alone."

I've come to see the wisdom of Verne's words. We all need someone in our corner we can trust, someone who can help us work through our deepest issues and blackest moments. Yes, coaches can be expensive. And yes, they can force us to look in the mirror at ourselves and our values, at what's working and what's not working in our lives. It can be a very humbling—and very grounding—experience.

Doing everything alone, not trusting anyone, not benefitting from other people's perspectives, can get leaders into a lot of trouble. I sometimes wonder what my father's life might have been like if he had been open to input or advice. Many years later and after speaking with other coaches, mentors and even shamans, I realized that my father had actually been an influential coach to me. If he had not been the person he is and done the things he did, I would not have learned from him who I needed to be. I would be a completely different person than I am today.

They say it takes a village to raise a child. I think it takes a village to raise a successful entrepreneur. Gradually, I was getting to see more and more of the people who belonged in my village: my wife and children, friends and peers at YEO and GOT, advisors and coaches. I had no inkling that even more extraordinary people would show up as I kept exploring what might be possible if I gave more of myself.

Gathering of Titans - Boston, USA (2014)

CHAPTER 8

Innovate or Die

Things had taken off after we signed the deal with Alyeska Pipeline Service Company in Alaska in 1994. For about five years after that, we had a good run with our technology. When our distributor FOSS expanded their operations overseas, they used our systems for their own work in regions from Indonesia to Azerbaijan.

But then things started to slow down. Competitors had caught on to what we were doing and were trying to emulate our RBS skimming systems. We needed something new: we needed to keep evolving our technology further. So I asked LP if we could increase the capacity of our skimmers, make them larger with higher recovery rates, maybe even invent a three-sided machine. Once again, he laughed at me until he saw I meant what I said. Then it was, "No way!"

And yet again, LP came through for us. After a few weeks, he called me into the back room to show me the basic three-sided machine he had built. I didn't hesitate to tell him that I could sell these machines. Within a few minutes, I was on the phone with Larry and Joe at FOSS, telling them of our new design. Off we went in a rush again, selling more and more product and building like crazy. And now LP had caught the bug.

Next there was the RBS 25, our first four-sided machine. Then there came a larger version called the RBS 40. After these two new models were selling all over the world, we developed the RBS 50, the largest of them all. Then we received a request through one of FOSS's contacts from the Abu Dhabi National

Oil Company (ADNOC): they wanted an even larger four-sided system than what we had available. We agreed to build one specifically for them and, in doing so, gave birth to our large-capacity, four-sided skimming system.

All this innovation was good. Evolving our technology was good. Yet I noticed that, for some reason, we were now losing out on contracts with international governments and government-owned oil companies.

Because of this I started making inquiries with several international government purchasing agencies to find out what was going on. Apparently, their requirements were evolving. Some governments had been having issues with the quality of products they had been receiving from international suppliers. Many of them had begun enforcing ISO standards and requiring that equipment be tested by third-party witnesses. Now these governments would only purchase from ISO-certified companies (those whose quality control was certified by the International Standards Organization) that had their equipment tested to an ASTM standard by a third-party witness. We met none of these new requirements. Our larger British and Danish competitors had international recognition and ISO certifications. Even though they were slower than we were at making decisions, changing course and developing new products, they were scooping up most of the international government contracts, leaving us in their wake.

At about this same time, our agent in Korea called to tell me that the entire Korean oil spill response regime was to be retooled. He insisted that, in order for Aqua-Guard to bid on these contracts, we would have to submit test certificates for all our machines. Each certificate had to be verified by either an international witness body, such as the American Bureau of Shipping, or DNV GL, a world-leading testing and certification company for the energy sector based in Norway.

Once more I made the trek from my desk back to LP's office to tell him what was happening and what we had to do. He listened to me until at one point, he just said, "Stop! Stop! This is *ridiculous*. You keep coming in here asking me for stuff. I keep doing it—but it is *never enough*."

I agreed. He was right. "And...," I insisted quietly, "...if we want to keep ahead of the curve, we need to do this." I knew that if we had these test certificates we could leverage them for many more potential contracts around the world, effectively forcing our competition out.

But this time LP was emphatic. "It is too much of a hassle. It's cost-prohibitive. Not this time. No. I am not going to do this."

I didn't know how to respond. I understood his concern. But I saw things differently. I understood the potential we were sitting on. We needed to keep our innovations at the forefront of the industry. We needed tools to keep ahead of the competition. Test certificates were one of those tools. That meant we really needed our equipment tested and certified right away. How could I help LP see what I saw?

Although email was the new medium of choice for business communications, I still believed there was no substitute for personal contact. So I had made it a point to meet in person with all our agents and as many of our clients as I could to keep my finger on the pulse of the industry. LP, on the other hand, didn't like to travel, so it was often hard to convey to him what I had seen and witnessed overseas.

Korea was a country where I had recent first-hand knowledge of client needs and concerns. I went back to our agent in Seoul and asked him to prepare some projections for me. We had just returned from visiting customers all over the country and so our data would be current. I wanted to know exactly what potential sales could go to whom over what period of time. He came back with a massive list. Most of the sales would go to Korea's "Big 5". These were the companies that controlled all the manufacturing and movement of oil to, from and around Korea. The national government had mandated them, along with the Korean Marine Pollution Response Corporation (KMPRC), to upgrade all their oil spill response capabilities.

This could be huge.

I walked back into LP's office with this data in hand. It took only a few minutes to persuade him to do the testing.

We set up our own tank and called in an independent observer from the American Bureau of Shipping to witness our tests and make sure we followed the ASTM standards exactly. Our test results turned out to be fantastic. We were able to turn around and bid on almost every project coming out of Korea related to marine oil spill response for the next several years. We bid on everything requiring small, medium and large skimmers. We bid on jobs requiring oil boom systems, reels and boats. We bid on anything that needed everything for spill response. And because we had our test certificates, we were able to win many of the contracts.

That one decision to take a chance and test our machines correctly, a decision based on actual hard data, proved to be the right one. This gave us the edge over our slower, larger competitors. With certificates in hand, we turned our ability to innovate and adapt quickly into lucrative contracts.

We had dodged the bullet again. But I was beat. Through all this, I had been burning the candle at both ends. I couldn't remember when I last saw my wife and kids. For almost 20 years, I had been away from home for up to six weeks at a time. Traveling, always traveling. I would start in northern Asia in Japan, Korea or China and work my way down through Hong Kong, Taiwan and Singapore to Manila, Bangkok, Kuala Lumpur and Jakarta, ending up in Sydney and Melbourne in Australia.

One day early in 2000 Sue put through a call to me in my office and said, "It's a Paco on the phone for you from South America." When I answered, he introduced himself to me in broken English and said he was an agent representing an American competitor of ours in Venezuela. He was sick of dealing with the American company as the quality of their product was extremely poor. He told me that ever since he had seen our RBS skimmers working in the field he had wanted to sell them for us. Now he wanted to be our agent in Venezuela.

Latin America, where I had spent time in my early 20s, had been dead to us for the past decade. Although we had done some pieces of work in Venezuela and Brazil during that time, we had focused on developing our main market in Asia. Now we needed someone to help develop this region. I knew that I was tapped out and that expansion into South America would be too much for me to take on alone.

After a long discussion with Paco, I hired him on the spot. Eventually, he opened an office for us in Miami, Florida and sold our products throughout Latin America. In time, he moved to Vancouver and became our regional manager for all of the Latin American region. In this new role, he did what I had been doing for years: traveling to a region, meeting and appointing agents/distributors, and, most of all, visiting clients in person. This not only helped expand our sales network, but also took pressure off me to be on the road so much. The strategy worked so well that within a few years I hired regional managers for Asia, Europe, the Middle East and Africa as well.

Meanwhile, Paco quickly opened the door for us in Venezuela, Brazil and Mexico. Within a very short period, he sold eight very large, four-sided RBS 50 machines to Pemex, Mexico's state-owned petroleum company. These machines were to be placed around the Gulf of Mexico for use in the event of a large offshore spill. Pemex drove a hard bargain. The payment terms they pushed on us were tough. In the end, our profit margins were slimmer than we wished, but we now had a foot in the newly expanding Mexican market.

Back in Vancouver, our 2,300-square-foot office and warehouse space was bursting at the seams. It was far too small for us. As a stop-gap measure, we had temporarily rented similar spaces beside our office. But now it was time to have a place of our own, one space that fit our needs and that we could hold as an asset on the books. In between traveling and closing deals, I began looking.

One day in 2003, our real estate agent called me and said, "Nigel, I may have something for you guys. Perhaps it is a bit big for you now...but the location is ideal and you can rent the upstairs for the time being if you don't need it."

I went to take a quick look and loved the place. But he was right. The building was far too large for what we needed right then. I went back to LP and suggested, "Let's go together and take a peek." The next thing I knew, we were signing an agreement to purchase the whole property.

I suppose I shouldn't have been surprised with the speed at which this happened. After all, I had been working my way through my asteroid belt with my coach Kevin. The more I cleared away, the faster the decisions were getting. I was finding that making a decision was better than not making one at all, even if it turned out to be the wrong one.

I have to say that buying this building was one of the best decisions we ever made. The real estate agent was correct: we were easily able to lease the upstairs while we rented out the downstairs to our operating company. Later, when we needed to, Aqua-Guard expanded into the top floor. Meanwhile, the value of the building kept rising.

That extra square footage gave us space for our ideas and our business to grow.

About a year before we moved into our commercial property, LP had started mentoring a protégé, a young fellow named Cameron Janz. Cam had worked with our guys and was rising through the ranks quickly. As a protégé, he pushed LP to stay at his creative edge and design newer and greater equipment.

I will never forget the day when LP and Cam came through the door from our new warehouse into our office and together invited me to see something. I stepped into the warehouse and saw the test tank was set up with one of our RBS skimmers floating in oil. They told me to watch. The brush started turning, but this time the amount of oil the system was recovering was visually a lot more that I had ever seen. I looked at them in amazement and asked, "What have you guys done?"

We had been having some difficulty in Alaska recovering heavy oil in some situations. Our RBS skimmers only had one scraper per brush and it was mounted in front. Recovered oil would have to flow by gravity through the system to a pump: in cold weather, this would, at times, get plugged up. They had come up with an idea to scrape the rotating brush with more than one scraper, plus they had installed a concentration plate underneath. A back scraper would peel off the heavy oil and put it directly into the pump. They told me that their calculations showed we could potentially recover 300% more oil with these innovations than we had previously with our RBS skimmers. I was blown away.

After having seen positive business outcomes with the tests of our RBS skimmers for the Korean market, it was easy to sell LP on verifying this machine with ABS or DNV. So Cam and LP set up a test. Their calculations were correct and our new skimmer was able to recover 300% more than the older RBS, while operating at our standard 98% efficiency. We needed a new name for this upgrade and decided that, with our water focus, we would call it "Triton", after the Greek god who stilled the waves.

We quickly applied for both U.S. and Canadian patents, which we were granted. Now we really had something that could differentiate us from any competition. I had also replicated myself several times with these new regional managers. Before we knew it, we had our skimmers in 104 countries around the world.

Aqua-Guard offshore skimmer - Japan (2012)

Meanwhile, my YEO buddy David Ash was busy buying up commercial real estate all over Vancouver, some properties for investments and some for his philanthropic endeavors. As soon as he heard that I had bought a building, he called me up to give me his advice. "Nigel, never sell your real estate. Keep it and hold it for the long run." Fortunately, I did—and I've never regretted doing so.

Dave was influencing me in other ways too. I was still looking at giving more of myself and being more engaged, but I really didn't know where to contribute beyond what we had done with Street Mom a few years back. I watched as Dave sold his business and started to ramp things up in the philanthropic space to focus on giving back to communities. During one of our Entrepreneur's Organization meetings (we no longer considered ourselves "young"), he mentioned that he had just come back from a life-changing experience in Mexico where he and his family had been building homes for the homeless. Curious, I asked him a *lot* of questions about what made the whole adventure "life-changing" for him. He answered, and then asked me if I would like to go with him to Mexico myself the next year and bring my family. Although the idea of building homes for the homeless intrigued me, the group Dave had been volunteering with was Christian-based and, to be honest, that freaked me out. I really didn't want to take my family somewhere to get hit over the head with a bible. So I politely declined.

As the dates for their next trip drew closer, my curiosity about the details of the journey and the build itself kept growing. Dave told me that they planned to fly to San Diego, California and then travel in a convoy of white vans south across the border with Mexico into Tijuana. There they would stay, heading out each morning to a location somewhere in the hills surrounding the border city to build a home for one of the families currently living there in shanties. Many of these families had migrated north from southern Mexico for an opportunity to work on an assembly line in a big American-owned factory just inside the border with the United States. Their pay was far less than what we would consider to be "minimum wage" in Canada, and most migrant workers arrived with very little resources, if any, for building a home.

Now he had my attention. I loved adventure. I couldn't change the system that had created this social injustice, but I could help address it, if only for one family. From what Dave told me, the group he had gone with had been building homes for the homeless for years, so I knew we would be in good hands. Perhaps if I took the family and kept an open mind on the whole Christian thing, this might be just what I was looking for. Dylan was eight, Devon was six, and Kina was three at the time. I talked it over with Rieko. We agreed to give it a try and take all our kids with us.

So one day in May 2003, we flew into San Diego airport with our three small children. Just outside the arrivals area, we found a row of white vans proudly bearing simple paper signs in their front windows: "Youth with a Mission" (YWAM). The drivers were yelling out, "All family members stay together in each van. Keep your passports ready for Mexican customs agents." Once each of us had loaded our single luggage bags into the back of the van, the caravan headed south to the Mexican border at the end of the I-5 highway.

We made one stop before Mexico for our last all-American burger at an In-N-Out. As I was climbing into the front seat opposite the driver with my Animal® Style Burger, I overheard him make one last check-in with the YWAM base in San Diego. "I have all the Bennett Baptists here and we are heading to TJ."

> *"The Bennett Baptists?" Oh boy. They think we are a church group. This is going to be interesting.*

At the border, the lineup was massive. From the front of the van, I looked out over a sea of wrecks, all types and shapes of old cars, most of them filled with itinerant Mexican workers, crossing back into Mexico. The traffic was controlled by a signal light that either turned green or red as you approached. If you got a red light, then you had to pull over to the side and the military police, their faces covered by bandanas to protect their identity and their fingers resting on the triggers of their AK-47s, would search your car. We were lucky and pulled a green. We slowly inched our way straight through the border, passing others who had not been so lucky and who were being interrogated by these intimidating masked men. And then it hit me.

We're passing into one of the most dangerous places on earth. Kidnappings and murders happen here everyday. The drug cartels run Tijuana and most of the border towns.

My heart began to race.

> *What am I doing bringing my young family to a place like this? Am I crazy? What have I done?*

Our driver seemed unperturbed by the military. He moved us slowly along the broken road, passing a sign that cheerfully welcomed us to the country. "Bienvenidos a México". There beside the greeting rose the largest Mexican flag I have ever seen, lazily waving in the breeze atop its 150-foot flagpole. What greeted us next gave me shivers.

We drove up over an overpass. Into view came a gigantic moat running between Mexico and the United States. On the far side of the moat stood a huge wall with razor wire running along the top. After that wall, there were multiple others, all barring exit from Mexico and entry into the States. I turned around in my seat to find Rieko and the kids all glued to their windows, eyes wide open and focused on this strange new world and what was going on outside the van.

As we drove through Tijuana, we passed beggars selling everything from figurines of Jesus to piñatas to churros. There were hundreds of people, some missing limbs, others without eyes, almost all desperately begging us through forced smiles to purchase something, anything from them.

After about 30 minutes of winding our way through this sea of poverty, we climbed a hill to a more open road that paralleled the border. From here, we could see the U.S. side, where Black Hawk helicopters patrolled back and forth along the wall. At one point, we slowed down and I could see ahead of us on the road a bunker made from sandbags, stocked with bandana-wrapped soldiers, their machine gun scopes reflecting in the sun. At the top of the mound of sandbags sat one soldier with a large 50 cal machine gun pointing right at us. As we drove up to the checkpoint, a soldier signaled us to stop. He leaned toward our driver's window to ask some questions in Spanish. My body tensed and I could feel the adrenaline surging through my veins.

> *This reminds me of my hasty escape from Egypt. I swore to myself I would never repeat that experience again...and here I have unknowingly recreated it, only this time for my whole family....*

I listened hard. My Spanish was passable, but not that great. I understood most of what he said. He was asking the driver where we were going and how many people we had in our van. The driver explained we were "gringos here to help the poor". The soldier nodded and indicated we could move on.

As we drove down the coast south of Tijuana, an overwhelming feeling of calm came over me, as if I'd just stepped into the eye of a storm. I knew I needed to be here—with my family. The "storm" was back home at Aqua-Guard, where things were getting thrown at us from all directions. I'd be returning to that storm soon enough. This time in Mexico—and whatever experiences we had here—would be a chance to connect with something bigger than just my company, an opportunity to start connecting with a much larger purpose.

Before I knew it, we had arrived at the humble YWAM base. Close quarters with six bunk beds to a room. I was amazed that the youth who came from all over the world to volunteer to build homes for the poor had to live in these conditions.

I will never forget our first build. We drove up into the hills on a dirt track, the heat beaming down on our old, thin-walled Ford van and the dust creeping through every open crack. We were met at the build site by Hector, the father, and his family of six, who were assembled at the entrance to their current "home" to greet us. A home that consisted of two old garage doors propped up in the dirt with a tarp slung between them to hold back the rain. A single wet, grimy mattress lay underneath. All seven of them were, literally, living in the dirt.

I was shocked. Hector was a proud young man. He, like many others before him, had come to Tijuana from southern Mexico looking for a better life for his family. This was their last resort, this hovel in a shanty town.

Hector considered himself lucky to be rich in terms of what really mattered to him. He had a job at a Panasonic factory nearby where he earned a few dollars a day. At the end of each shift, he would run the gauntlet of desperate thieves and drug cartels back to his squat. I don't think he realized that he was trapped in a living hell. And he wasn't the only one. Companies from America, Korea, Japan, China and Europe had set up factories along the border to take advantage of cheap labor. Millions of Mexicans were working in factories for a pittance and squatting in shanties in these border towns.

The home we were going to build for Hector and his family was going to be a castle in comparison. It would be a safe place they could lock up. Finally, they could go to sleep at night and not have to worry that everything they owned would be missing in the morning—or worse.

A few days prior to our arrival, other YWAM volunteers had poured a 16 by 20-foot concrete pad. Today, our team of 23 volunteers would begin building the frame for his castle. We introduced ourselves to the family, unloaded all the building materials from our vans, and then had a safety meeting. After organizing ourselves into three teams (trusses, gables and paint), we got to work. Rieko and Kina were on the paint team: Dylan, Devon and I would build trusses.

We all worked hard. No one in my family had any building experience. Thankfully, we had volunteer supervisors to teach us. Adan, a young, long-haired Mexican boy of 18, was our head supervisor. We found out later that he was the only son of a single mother. She herself did not live in a house and she had to raise Adan under very difficult circumstances.

Although he was poor in terms of worldly goods, Adan gave of himself to help those even less fortunate. For me, this was hard to grasp. Here was a young man with so little, and yet he was like the Pied Piper to all the kids on the build site. He was helping Dylan, Devon and Kina, giving them just the right amount of instruction so they were doing what they needed to do. He was teaching them how to hold a hammer and hit a nail, how to pull out a nail to try again when they missed, without them even blinking an eye. All the kids loved Adan.

If I had noticed what was going on with them sooner, perhaps I would have followed their lead and listened to Adan's instructions. I hadn't swung a hammer for years and, within a few hours, my hands were raw and blistered. By the end of day one, the sun had taken its toll on me: I had developed a massive headache. And yet, it was satisfying to look around the site and see the progress we had made.

Even more amazing were our kids. Rieko and I stood back and watched in disbelief. Were these really our children? At home, it was tough just to get them up in the morning to go to school and they would constantly fight amongst themselves. But here, they were working together as a team, helping each other, hammering and painting with purpose. Three-year-old Kina tried her hand at hammering in nails but was missing most times. When she did make contact, she would bend the nail. Each time this happened, either Dylan or Devon would help her pull out the nail and try again. We couldn't believe our eyes.

By the end of the day, it didn't really matter that we were tired. The joy of nailing the last shingle on the roof and putting the last touches of paint on the walls was uplifting. We formed a circle in the dirt outside Hector's family's new home. Kina, all covered in paint, dust and dirt, had a huge smile on her face as she gazed up at me. Rieko, Dylan and Devon, similarly covered, were beaming as well. When we passed the keys of the home to the mother, Rieko broke down in tears. And then we all did. We knew what awaited her and her family.

We all stood and watched as she turned the key in the lock and then slowly opened the door. Expecting to enter an empty home, she screamed with delight when she saw what was inside. Then she started to shake and cry with joy at the surprise we had arranged for them.

A few hours earlier, we had arranged for some of the ladies in the volunteer crew to take the whole family shopping with a small sum of money we had donated for that purpose. While they were away, we had filled the new house with furniture, set up drapes, assembled bunk beds for the kids and laid the table for dinner. The finishing touch: we scattered toys across the beds.

Homes of Hope - Mexico

We let the family enter their new home and close the door. After several minutes, Kina went to knock on the door to ask their permission to enter. When I stepped inside and saw Hector's face, I grabbed him and we hugged and cried together in joy for a minute or so. While we had been working together on the trusses, he had told me of his family and their hardships. It was hard for me to comprehend, but Hector was now the first of his entire bloodline to live in a home.

This was one of the most impactful and meaningful experiences of my life. To have my wife and children experience it with me was magic.

CHAPTER 9
Ups & Downs

After returning from Homes of Hope in Mexico, I stopped the car at the top of our driveway in Vancouver and looked at our own home through fresh eyes.

> *This is not right. Why do we have so much and so many in the world have so little?*

And then from the back seat, our kids piped up with a question that resonated with us both. "When can we go again?" Followed by a surprising, "And next time, can we bring a friend?" Within a week, our entire family had agreed that we would rather go to Homes of Hope every year than go on a vacation in some beautiful place like Hawaii.

After our third year of running the gauntlet of the Mexican border, our kids agreed to do presentations to their school classes about their adventures building homes for the homeless. What happened next was quite miraculous.

Kina and Devon were still pretty little, so Rieko went with Kina and I went with Devon. When their classmates saw our kids in the slide shows, they instantly connected with what was going on. Suddenly, all the hands in the room went up. One child after another asked us, "Why don't those kids have houses?" "Why..." "Why...?" "Why?" The chorus was loud.

The classic question came to Devon. "How much do they pay you to go down and do this?" I will never forget the look on my young son's face. He was perplexed at first, and then I could see him figure out his reply. "Why would anyone pay us to do such a nice thing? We don't get paid anything. It's just a nice thing to do."

That evening at home, Rieko and I compared notes from what we had witnessed with each class. The engagement of the kids was amazing. Then at 5:30 p.m. the phone started ringing. And ringing. And ringing. One by one, the parents of the kids who had seen Kina and Devon's presentations were calling to see if they could come with us on our next trip to Mexico. We were blown away. Our answer was that we just attended the trips: they were organized by this Christian group and we actually didn't lead or organize them. In every single case, the parents half asked us, half told us that if "we" would organize and lead a trip, they would surely come.

Rieko and I were so dumbfounded that we called YWAM the next day and spoke to a representative. That person put us in touch with Sean Lambert, the founder of Homes of Hope. When he heard our story, he said to us, "Nigel and Rieko, thank you so much for coming and giving of yourselves and your family. I know that you guys aren't Christians. You have given of yourselves and are educating your kids in the best way possible. What you are doing means much more than just going to church on a Sunday and making a donation. You are welcome to come any time and bring as many volunteers as you can to help build homes for the less fortunate. You and they will always be welcome. We appreciate you and your friends so much."

His words made me feel much better about the whole religious side of things. And so we notched up our commitment by agreeing to organize and lead a group of interested families to Mexico. Sean asked Carey, a representative from Calgary, to speak to our group in Vancouver. We organized an information session at our house in North Vancouver and were flabbergasted at the turnout: 50 people showed up. Carey did a short presentation and we shared stories of our experiences building.

Fifty people were a lot to take on our first group, but we anticipated that only half of those who expressed interest would actually go. Over the next few days, the phone kept ringing and ringing. We ended up with a group of 80 people, consisting of parents along with young kids, all who were fully committed to going. We couldn't take everyone all at once, so we had to split up the group and do three trips.

I got a lot more satisfaction out of leading these trips with my family than out of any business deal I had done. They were life-changing events not only for the people we built homes for, but also for the families who came with us to build. Every trip was a chance for us to connect with things that really matter, to re-ground ourselves, to take time out and be in the calm eye of our own individual life "storms".

It snowballed from there. The energy just kept growing, not just for us, but for almost everyone we came in contact with. Our kids and their friends kept coming to Mexico year after year, sometimes two or three times a year, returning every time to give presentations to their classes. Over the next few years, our network of house-building volunteers kept growing. Some people even split off to form new groups heading to Central America, South America and Africa.

The snowball kept rolling.

Our family sponsored several foster children in Ecuador, Pakistan and Africa. We started volunteering on Christmas mornings with David Ash's family to serve lunch to people on Vancouver's East Side at the Dodson Hotel. Run by a foundation, the converted hotel provides homeless people in the area with access to affordable housing, addictions and medical assistance, housekeeping and employment services and a community kitchen program.

It's now 2017 and our family has led over 700 volunteers, mostly families, on 18 trips to Mexico to build homes for the homeless. Our kids are now in their 20s and, in spite of their busy lives, they still make sure we are booked to go every year. Their friends also call to make sure we are booked. Year after year, all these young people keep saying they would rather go to Mexico to build homes for the homeless than go to a beach resort. That means a lot to us.

It looked as if things at work were actually going well when we started into 2008. Aqua-Guard seemed to be on the right track with our technology, our sales and our property.

And then the stock market crashed. Capital spending stopped. Funding for equipment to safeguard against environmental disasters dried up.

Our revenues slowed to a crawl and, to make things even worse, one Saturday morning near the end of the year, I got a call from our external accountant Garnet. There was something in his voice that immediately put me on alert. "Look, Nigel," he told me. "I've been working on your year-end financials and no matter what way I look at the numbers, they don't seem right. I know it's the weekend, but I really need to see you about this—right away."

Responding to the urgency in his voice, I agreed to meet him at a restaurant in Burnaby that afternoon. When Garnet arrived, he immediately pulled out the financial statements to show me. He said, "We are short almost a million."

I looked at him, perplexed. "Not possible," was my immediate reaction. "Our CEO has his finger on the pulse of the business...and our CFO couldn't be wrong...right?"

Garnet told me again that the numbers were off, adding, "That's not all. There is also $75,000 missing."

My face must have told it all right then. He went on, "I fear that our CFO has been moving funds from the company into his personal holding account."

I couldn't believe what I was hearing.

Worst of all, I couldn't do anything with Garnet's suspicions. We needed real proof.

I took a deep breath and called our CEO at the time to discuss the situation. He became extremely agitated. I could tell how angry he was by how loudly he spoke—and this was the loudest I had ever heard him. I felt he knew this fell on his watch and that, ultimately, he would have to go. I asked him to meet us at the company office right away.

We arrived and immediately began to look for evidence. After a few hours, we finally found out how the CFO had transferred the funds: he had hacked one of our bank widgets. He had also issued checks in erasable ink. He would fill in a check to a supplier, get us to sign the check, then erase the payee and make it payable to his holding company. We found enough evidence to prove that this had been going on for seven months.

We had everything we needed.

The next morning at 7:00, I met our CEO, LP and Cam (who was now running most of our operations and held a very important seat on our bus) at the office so we could greet our CFO before the other employees arrived. When he came through the door at his regular (now suspiciously early) 7:30 arrival time, we confronted him about the discrepancies in the financials. At 8:00 am, the police showed up—right on cue—and took him away. He later did three years in prison.

But that wasn't the worst of it. We were not just short the $75,000 he had embezzled. Our books were all wrong and we were actually $900,000 in the hole. We were weeks away from our year end and we needed to report our financials to the bank. When the bank heard what had happened, they threatened to pull our line of credit, which we were deeply into at the time.

We did some further investigation and found that our CFO and his wife had been living quite a high life and operating behind a façade. His peers knew him as a high-flying fellow. His extravagant lifestyle caused him to always need more and more, to the point where he became stuck and, in his mind, felt that he had to steal from us. This was a completely different mindset and culture than what we were building in Aqua-Guard. Our focus was on providing for our families, taking care of our employees and creating a company that contributed to keeping the world's oceans clean.

That alignment of values and company culture really came into play now. I remember Cam coming into my office the day we found out the bank wanted to pull our line of credit and telling me he could help prepare a financial report that we could take to them to prove that we were good for our loan. We cleared the decks so he could focus for the next few days on preparing a massive binder full of financial information for that purpose. Thankfully, Cam had been much closer to the numbers than either our CEO, LP or I had and knew what work we had in the pipeline that was certain.

When we met with Dean, our Vancouver bank manager, to explain the situation, we were able to present a solid case. Although he was our bank manager, we saw him as a key part of our external team and our community. Dean understood our situation and he truly wanted to help us succeed. But it was his boss in Toronto, Ontario who ultimately called the shots. Dean believed in us and agreed to fly to Toronto to explain our situation. Armed with everything we had prepared, Dean headed back east to plead our case directly with his boss. Apparently, that wasn't enough. The two of them invited us into a conference call to go over all the details they wanted clarified. We responded to the best of our ability.

Two weeks went by. Not a word. We were all sitting on tenterhooks. Then one afternoon, "Nigel, the phone is for you. It is Dean." My stomach tensed up as I went into my office to take the call. I picked up the phone receiver and tentatively said, "Hello?"

Dean sounded quite pleased. "Nigel, I have good news. The bank has agreed to give you guys more time. You have until Christmas to get things sorted out. There's one condition: we will need very accurate reports from you every week between now and then." I agreed, and told Dean we were very appreciative of him going to bat for us.

As soon as he heard the good news, Cam asked to talk to LP and I upstairs in our boardroom. LP and I both sat there waiting for him, still somewhat in shock, wondering what we could do next. The situation was dire. Our CFO was going to jail. Over the past few years, we had moved through three General Managers and CEOs. One we let go when the business seemed to outgrow him and his expertise. Another came from a large institution and wasn't used to rolling up their sleeves when needed. The other tended to bully our staff as opposed to work with them and so didn't fit our corporate culture.

Cam entered the board room, stepped up to our white board and just gave it to us straight.

"Look, guys, I can help turn this thing around. I have been here since I was 18. I've worked every facet of the business from shop floor and production to estimating and sales. I know *everything* that goes on here. We will have to cut—and we will have to cut deep—if we want to be here at Christmas. If you give me a chance, I can turn things around. Do you trust me to do that?"

> *I can't believe that LP and I didn't see this before. All the while we have been attempting to parachute in a leader as someone to drive our bus, we have been internally grooming someone to be the perfect fit. Unfortunately, it took a situation like this for us to actually see it.*

Both LP and I were done with leading operations. We trusted Cam and, without any hesitation, handed him the steering wheel. From that moment on, Cam would drive our bus, build the culture and run the day-to-day operations of the Aqua-Guard business.

I remember driving home that evening and thinking back to my first meetings with coach Kevin and how we had identified this overwhelming asteroid belt that I had to move through. Such a daunting task at the time.

The moment we handed ops to Cam I realized the value of all the challenges we had worked through—from breaking away from my father's company to risk starting a new business and the struggle to get and fulfill contracts to dealing overseas and eventually navigating through this betrayal. I realized that I needed to experience the pain of working through each and every asteroid. I needed to experience and learn from every pitch of the climb. I needed all these experiences—and all the learning that came with them. Everything on this path had been in preparation for me to be ready to, one day, trust someone like Cam to take the driver's seat. Everything had led me to being ready to step out of the day-to-day and into a more supportive role.

It was April 2009, and I was headed back to Boston and MIT for my Gathering of Titans session. I had been attending for a few years and, although I felt I was at the point of moving on from the group, one of the speakers, Simon Sinek, yanked me back. I was glad I went. His talk was riveting.

Simon focused entirely on one question: "Why?"

He asked us:

- Why are *we* here?
- Why do *you* do the things that you do?
- What is *your* "Why?"

At first, I had no idea what he was talking about. But then he explained two things. First, your "why" is the reason you do everything. Your why is your path. Second, how you do anything is how you do everything. I sat back and thought about how this applied to me and Aqua-Guard.

I was trying to re-invent my business. And I could re-invent it around a powerful "Why?"

I thought long and deep. Finally I got it. Aqua-Guard could be much more than an oil spill *response* equipment company. We had a massive platform in over 104 countries around the world. We were selling ourselves short. Our big "Why?" was actually "to protect the world's most precious resource". And that resource was water.

OMG! This had been right in front of me all the time. But I had always been so busy, nose to the grindstone, putting out fires in the business, that I never saw it. This 30,000-feet-high perspective helped me see into the heart of what was great about our company. That longing to protect the planet that I had felt at the beginning of my career. The sense of "guardianship" that had always been at the core of Aqua-Guard.

As soon as I got back to Vancouver, I met with coach Kevin. At our company's next quarterly meeting, I wanted to outline this new "Why?" along with a simple, one-page action plan. I knew what my partners and staff would think: they would look at me like I was crazy, coming back from MIT again with some new idea. I didn't want that to happen this time. This new "Why?" was much bigger than any of us. It was our Big Hairy Audacious Goal, as Verne Harnish would say. It was something huge to shoot for, something so huge we would have to push all limits to achieve it. Understandably, it would take time for everyone to buy into our new purpose, but it would gradually become part of our corporate culture.

After Cam officially took over as CEO at the end of 2008, we had decided to have a few sessions with Kevin and Aqua-Guard's entire management team to look at our big "Why?" and evaluate our one-page Rockefeller Habits action plan. In hindsight, I should have anticipated there might be a bit of tension in the room between LP and Kevin. It's tough for anyone to let someone else critique your baby. But I knew we needed this now more than ever.

I had been thinking deep and hard about our purpose. Why we did what we did was about what we wanted to protect. Water. Water means life on earth. No water, no life.

We were in the business of water protection. Then we really needed to hyper-focus to take things to the next level.

But focus where—and on what?

I had learned that when I or we hyper-focused on something, we were hugely successful. The problem now was, in order to get hyper-focused, we had to be pushed outside our comfort zone. It is just like climbing: routes will appear when you step outside that zone.

What might the next evolution of Aqua-Guard and our quest to protect the world's most precious resource be? Global oil demands were increasing, especially from countries like China. The sweet surface oil available in Venezuela and Texas that North and Central America had tapped into in the 1960s was all but gone. Oil was becoming harder and harder to get at. And more and more lucrative. With a barrel going for over $60, it was viable to go after more remote sources: exploration and production companies even in my own country were now venturing further offshore to drill deeper into the earth's crust and contemplating immense development projects like the Oil Sands in Northern Alberta.

I kept thinking about what would happen if there was another blowout or another massive spill far offshore. No equipment existed to contain or recover oil at this scale so far out at sea. I reflected back to the largest machines we had built so far: the ones for ADNOC in Abu Dhabi, the eight machines in Mexico, the equipment for Petrobras in Brazil. They had all been a larger version of our small RBS skimmers. What if we were able to go really big, even bigger than the Pemex Mexican machines? What if we could integrate our RBS skimming technology into a larger machine that could be dropped onto a vessel of opportunity and taken to a spill far offshore?

We knew this would be a very specific niche market. A market with little or no competition. The opportunity was huge. There would be high R&D (Research & Development) costs to get into the market, but if we did it right, the margins would be high. All we had to do was evolve our skimming technology.

The meeting with Kevin and our management team was perfect for sharing my thinking and deciding what direction we wanted to take with our big "Why?" After I walked everyone through what I was seeing, I shared that we had been getting indicators from our regional managers and clients in Brazil, Korea and Japan that this larger equipment was needed. I had an idea. But no client commits to just an idea. It seemed as if we were being thrown a hard ball. We could pack it all in and simply walk away from this opportunity. Or we could take the risk and put most of our eggs in this basket of "offshore oil spill response".

We all turned to look at LP. Because it all came down to the technology. He realized what we were thinking and cried out, "Not *again*!"

Cam chipped in and said, "Wait a minute, you guys. We have built all the components and sold them to various clients around the world. We know they all work. There's just one piece we have not supplied yet: a floating hose system that can be stored on one reel and that can recover oil from the skimmer and pump it right through the reel into a tank. It's true we have not done this...yet... but if we could, we could corner this market."

That insight turned the bigger vision of protecting the world's most precious resource from my Gathering of Titans class in Boston into a possibility. All we needed to do was pull this one rabbit out of the hat. For that to happen, we needed to find a solution to the floating hose issue and, once found, hyper-focus on getting the whole system to market.

We decided to design the heck out of this new "URO offshore oil skimming system". It would be like a real-life version of one of Hasbro's toy Transformers®: when powered up, it would come alive like a monster on the side of a ship and when compressed down, it would go back to sleep in its 20 by 8 by 12-foot shipping container and be on standby for the next event.

We worked with Kevin to lay out our goals on a one-page quarterly plan. This made things very simple: we could see what pieces had to be done, by whom and by when. We started biting off bits of work, one piece at a time. Our engineers worked on a design and drew up the plans in AutoCAD. We then passed this on to Paco, who started heavily marketing the system in South America, and to our regional manager Ron who did the same in Asia. As a company, we seemed to function better and with more clarity when all the chips were on the table and there was no turning back.

What happened next was unexpected.

CHAPTER 10
Drowning

We were just pulling ourselves out of sure bankruptcy in early 2009 when one of our largest competitors came knocking on the door.

Vikoma, the oldest oil spill equipment company on the planet, wanted to discuss a strategic alliance. We had been competing against Vikoma, our nemesis from the United Kingdom, on every international project since our inception. To form a strategic alliance with them would have been a good move for us at the time because, although we had supplied equipment to both Gulf Wars, they had a much stronger presence in the Middle East than we did.

Apparently, their new owners wanted to meet with us in New York, halfway between Vancouver and London. I agreed to fly to the Big Apple with the understanding we would be talking about forming a global alliance. But after five minutes of face-to-face discussion, it was apparent they didn't want an alliance: they wanted the whole thing. Their objective was to buy Aqua-Guard outright.

I was taken aback. I didn't want to sell the company after all we had been through. And so my response was immediate and clear: thank you for your interest but we are *not* for sale.

Back home in Vancouver, I told LP what had happened. He thought I was crazy not to entertain an offer from them. His annoyance with me lingered in the air between us for weeks. But that wasn't the end of it.

Within a month, one of Vikoma's two new owners was calling me up, asking me to reconsider. He threw a very large number out, a number that was hard to ignore. So I agreed to open up the discussion again if both owners would fly to Vancouver to propose a deal in person.

The meeting began in our boardroom with an offer for something less than what we had discussed on the phone. Right away, I asked for a private meeting with LP. We closeted ourselves in a nearby office. LP was still keen to sell, but I believed we could get a lot more for the business. I asked him to trust me. He pushed back, saying, "No, this is a good deal. Take it." I reassured him I could push for a higher price and told him to sit tight for a bit.

We returned to the boardroom, where I wasted no time in telling our potential buyers that their number was too low. They came back with a question: what number would be more appropriate? I upped the number by seven figures. They looked at each other and said they would have to talk about it. Now it was their turn to get up and leave the room.

An hour went by.

LP was angry: he told me that I had ruined the deal. "They will never pay that much for us!", he muttered. I quietly reassured him. "Let's wait and see. After all, we have nothing to lose. They want to buy us more than we want to sell."

Eventually, they returned and sat down on the other side of the boardroom table. The silence between us was deafening. And then a hand was extended.

"You have a deal."

All the blood drained from LP's face. We four all shook hands and agreed to draft up a letter of understanding and sign it before the Vikoma owners had to board their return flight to the U.K.

Over the next twelve months, I flew between Scotland, London, New York and Vancouver many times, working through due diligence matters and, eventually, preparing a final deal. But the more time that passed, the more the whole thing felt wrong to me. Aqua-Guard was *our* baby: we had started the company in 1992, built it up with our blood, sweat and tears, and now we were going to sell it for a big bag of cash. Then what? Sell t-shirts on the beach?

By April 2010, we had a non-refundable deposit in hand from Vikoma. But the legal side of the deal kept moving very slowly and it felt to me as if I was doing most of the work. We had been going back and forth for almost a year now and I was getting tired of the negotiations. Both LP and I were burned out from the roller coaster ride of simultaneously running and selling the business. In our minds, we had already sold and had "checked out" somewhat from being a daily driving force. Although I still had my doubts about selling, LP was still clear he wanted out. And so it was with some unease that I flew to Boston for my next Gathering of Titans session.

Escaping the airport, I grabbed a taxi out to Dedham where the MIT campus was located. It wasn't until we drove past the gates of Endicott House and into the parking lot that I realized I really didn't want to be there. I was tired. GOT, for me, felt like it had also run its course. An amazing annual conclave, but the speakers over the past few years seemed to focus only on business growth, financial gain, and the old entrepreneurial myth that if you are not growing, you are dying.

But my mood changed as soon as I ran into all my GOT brothers and sisters at our first event. Although we only saw each other four days a year, I was getting pretty tight with many of them. And I was eager to catch up with Gary, my good friend and roommate from Chicago.

I entered the theater with my colleagues and took a seat at the back of the room on the left. Two well-dressed women came and sat beside me, and we chatted cheerily until Rick, the moderator, started to speak.

Rick was an outspoken, gregarious character, quick with jokes and a real guy's guy. Normally he would enter, welcome everyone and launch into the roster of speakers. But this time, he shared the story of Brother David, an Austrian Jew and Benedictine monk who had survived the Holocaust and devoted his life to gratefulness. Rick's encounters with Brother David had obviously and profoundly changed him: instead of intimidating charisma, we now saw an unexpected sincerity. I was pleasantly surprised. Sipping my coffee, I glanced over at the lady beside me and smiled.

An 80-year-old man dressed in monk's robes stepped up to the podium. Brother David began speaking very softly, creating a sense of overwhelming calm in the room. I was suddenly all ears. And I wasn't alone. We all were riveted to his every word.

Brother David had just completed a year-long silent meditation. He shared his story of being drafted in Austria at the age of 14 by the German army just as WWII was beginning. The only person in his platoon to survive the killing field, he escaped from the army to find his parents and sister and saved them from being executed by the Nazis. He led their exodus to the United States, where he ended up studying philosophy. Over the years, he became a conduit for Buddhist-Christian dialogue and eventually founded The Gratefulness Institute. I was wowed by his words: "When you have death before your eyes, every day is great. You learn to live in the now."

I had been brought up to believe in only what I could witness first-hand. Other than Sunday school when I was very young, my parents had raised me outside of any religion or spirituality. My talk with David Ash at the Coronado Hotel and our trips to Mexico to help the homeless had started to soften me to alternative ways of thinking. And now this man who had endured unspeakable inhumanity and chosen gratefulness was showing me such strength in his vulnerability. I was keen to hear the next speaker.

Rick then introduced Lynne Twist, the author of *The Soul of Money*, who was currently working with indigenous tribes in the Amazon to help preserve their way of life via an organization she had formed with her husband called the Pachamama Alliance. He spoke of how she had been a global executive for the international Hunger Project working to end world hunger, and how she had worked with Mother Teresa in India. He then looked directly at one of the ladies sitting beside me and said, "Please welcome Lynne Twist." Over the sound of loud applause, the elegant, 60-year-old woman sitting right beside me stood up, touching my shoulder lightly as she passed on her way to the podium.

Lynne thanked Rick for the introduction. And then the room went silent, as if we had been waiting for someone like this to come and speak to us.

She opened with a concept that resonated with me: the idea of leading a meaningful life, a life committed to leaving the planet better than we found it.

She discussed her initial meeting with Mother Teresa in India, their eventual working relationship, her work in Ethiopia after the famine of 1983-1984, and her experiences running the Hunger Project globally. She candidly shared how she was run ragged traveling from India to Africa with this work and back to North America to raise her young family.

In 1995, John Perkins, author of the partly autobiographical best-selling book *Confessions of an Economic Hit Man** and a dear friend of Lynne's, invited her to go on a trip with him into the mountains of Guatemala to meet with the elders

....

* John Perkins, *Confessions of an Economic Hit Man* (San Francisco, CA: Berrett-Koehler Publishers, 2004).

of an indigenous tribe. John, a former Peace Corps volunteer in Latin America and the Middle East, had been seconded by a U.S. government corporation and trained to help coax many foreign governments—from Panama and Iran to Ecuador and Indonesia, but most of all Saudi Arabia—to take on massive loans to build infrastructure in their countries. These loans, often designed to ensure natural resources like oil would keep flowing to North America, left the countries in debt and under the influence of the United States. John referred to this work as that of an "economic hit man". This was completely opposite to his morals, so he eventually left it behind and began to help indigenous tribes preserve their way of life by keeping Big Oil out of the Amazon rainforest.

At that time, Lynne had never been to Latin America. She knew no Spanish. She was very busy. But John insisted. And so she agreed to meet him in Guatemala City and travel with him from there into the Mayan Highlands.

She explained that a Mayan shaman led her through a ceremony unlike anything she had ever experienced before. She was put into a trance: her vision was of flying like a large bird over the Amazon, looking down through the canopy of the rainforest to the earth and glimpsing brightly painted faces raised to greet her. These people were all wearing headdresses made of black, red and yellow feathers and speaking a language she didn't recognize.

Amazingly, Lynne's vision resonated completely with John. In fact, John had recently been in the Amazon and knew that the Achuar, a dream culture, were asking for contact and felt this vision was coming from them. It became clear to John that this was a call that needed to be answered and told Lynne, "We need to go to them. I know who they are. I know where they are. These are the Achuar people."

While working with a tribe called the Shuar in the Ecuadorian rainforest, John had heard of an enemy tribe called the Achuar who had not yet made contact with the outside world. John insisted that the vision meant they had to go and meet the Achuar. Lynne shrugged it off, saying she just had no time. She was far too busy and had to be in Africa the following week for a Hunger Project board meeting.

So Lynne returned to her husband, Bill, and her home in San Francisco and from there traveled on to Africa. But the images of the painted faces haunted her dreams at night. And when Lynne sat down in the board meeting in Africa and looked around the table, the faces of all the participants slowly started morphing into the painted faces of the people she had envisioned in the rainforest. She thought she was going crazy. So she excused herself from the board meeting and returned to the States for a rest.

Back in San Francisco, her visions and dreams continued. Bill had to go to San Diego for a business trip for his highly successful yacht design company: he left Lynne resting at home. But Bill kept thinking about what was happening. A few days later, he called to tell his wife that he had changed his mind: she *had* to go to the Amazon—and he would go with her. They would meet up with John Perkins and somehow find the Achuar.

The two of them flew into Quito, the capital of Ecuador, where they connected with John and his friend, Daniel Koupermann. Daniel, son of a French father and an Ecuadorian mother, had been raised in Ecuador and worked there as a physical and spiritual guide. After traveling together for several days in a four-wheel drive, the four reached the edge of the Amazon headwaters, where they met a Shuar pilot who agreed to fly them in a small plane into Achuar territory. After landing beside the Pastaza River, they disembarked and were greeted by faces with yellow, red and black headdresses coming out from the rainforest. These were the exact same faces Lynne had seen in her dreams.

Speaking through a translator, the Achuar people said, "You have come! We have been calling out to you. We knew that contact with the outside world would be inevitable. We wanted to initiate contact and have the right people come to work with us to help preserve our way of life." The meeting that followed led to the formation of the Pachamama Alliance by Lynne, Bill, John and Daniel.

Pachamama in their Achuar language means "Mother Earth, the sky, the universe and all time". This Pachamama Alliance, with a mandate to preserve the world's tropical rainforests by empowering the indigenous peoples who are their natural custodians, would be a bond between many indigenous tribes of the Amazon and leaders in contemporary society. The Achuar elders requested that the four co-founders return home and literally "change the dream of the modern world".

Lynne announced to our Titans class that she was leading a trip deep into the Amazon rainforest of Ecuador that May. If any of us wanted to join her, we were more than welcome. She asked for a show of hands. I didn't even think twice: I raised my hand to the roof.

Her talk turned everything I had learned about the purpose of money and business on its head. Here I was, in the middle of selling my business and about to grab the cash. And here was this amazing woman, standing in front of us and demonstrating that there is another way.

I had read *The Soul Of Money* just before coming to GOT and had been reflecting on it with regard to the acquisition of Aqua-Guard by the British company.

Many of the ideas Lynne discussed in the book were starting to resonate with me. The idea that money can be toxic to many people of wealth, giving them a distorted opinion of themselves and their worth. The idea of reallocating wealth streams to help them and their families cut back on the conspicuous consumption of their lives. The idea that people who live in poverty may be poor in terms of financial assets, but rich in creativity, courage and innovation (the "rich poor").

Lost in thought, I almost missed Lynne's thank you to our class. As she made her way back to her seat, I stepped out into the aisle. As she approached, I extended my arms out to hug her, quickly whispering in her ear that her talk was one of the most influential I had ever heard and that I wanted to join her in the Amazon in May. The only problem was we were leading another trip to Mexico at that exact same time. As she sat down beside me, I asked if there was another trip coming up that I could join.

"There is a CEO fundraiser in August you could attend," she replied.

"Great," I said. "I will come under one condition: that I am able to bring my family with me."

She explained that this particular trip was for CEOs only, and that there were just twelve spots.

But I persisted. "I believe the youth of the world are the ones who can make real change. So it's very important for me to bring my kids.... We are at the top of our curve but the youth are just at the beginning of theirs. They have the potential to return home from a journey like this and inform their friends of what they experienced, post about it on social media and become champions of the cause." I had seen happen this firsthand with our kids talking about their Homes of Hope experiences with their peers and classmates.

She looked intently at me, then slowly smiled—and gave me a massive hug.

For the next few days, I was on such a high that I couldn't even focus. All I could think about was gratefulness, living in the moment, and our upcoming Amazon journey. On the final evening of the GOT session, Brother David joined our entire class for dinner in a local restaurant. At one point, I felt compelled to walk over and ask if I could hug him. He smiled in agreement. As I embraced him, I began crying like a baby. He consoled me, "Let it all out." When the tears were over, I felt like I was reborn. I told him how grateful I was to have met my wife, to have three amazing kids and to have him appear in my life at just the right time.

The next morning I flew to Chicago to meet up with Rieko for a few days of R&R. We went for dinner that evening and all I could talk about was Brother David and Lynne Twist. I told Rieko our family had been invited by Lynne to go deep into the Amazon to meet with a tribe that had only had contact with the outside world for the past few years through her Pachamama Alliance. The trip was scheduled for August, only three months away. I could tell Rieko thought I was totally crazy. I brought up the fact that our kids were becoming fanatical about BBC's documentary film series *Planet Earth*, narrated by David Attenborough. Again, my amazing wife agreed to come on an adventure with me and to bring our kids. This time round Dylan was 16, Devon was 14 and Kina was 10.

As soon as we arrived back home in Vancouver, we asked all three kids if they wanted to go on a journey that summer deep into the jungle of Ecuador to meet a tribe of people that had very little contact with the outside world. Not only were they pretty stoked to go. They thought we were crazy to even ask. It was a unanimous chorus of "Yes!!!"

The last time I had been to South America had been the year before in 2009. Paco, our regional manager, and I had been traveling through Brazil for several weeks on a whirlwind sales tour. We would meet with our agents well into the night regarding strategy, then visit with our clients during the day in the municipalities of Niterói, Macaé and Angra all around the state of Rio de Janeiro, as well as Santos in the state of São Paulo.

With the first weekend came our first break. Paco was a surfer: he had been riding the waves before he could walk. Being raised in Venezuela, it was normal for him to get up at 5:00 a.m. on the weekend and head to the coast to surf—even in winter. I too loved to be in the water, although I was not that good a surfer. I had only started the sport when I was 40. But we both felt the ocean calling us.

The weather was terrible. No matter. We booked into a small hotel on the beach in Barra da Tajuca, located in the westernmost region of Rio de Janeiro. From there, we grabbed a taxi to take us south along the coast road to look for a spot to surf. From the safety of the car, we watched the rain coming down in sheets, we heard the wind howling, and we saw the waves pummeling the coastline. At one point, we asked the driver to stop the taxi to let us view the raging ocean from the top of a cliff. Paco looked at the waves, then at me and said, "Let's go!"

Cameron Janz supervising spill response - Venezuela (c2007)

We jumped back into the cab and drove a few more minutes to the next large inlet. The middle of Grumari Bay looked like a massive washing machine, with waves frothing with white water everywhere. As usual, I was craving adventure. This time I'd get my fix by paddling out in a full storm.

We stepped out into the warm rain and walked through the wet sand to a seemingly abandoned hut and a tanned, weather-beaten, thirty-year-old guy who was sitting under its cover. Paco knowingly informed me, "He's a surfer."

"Oi Tudo Bem," Paco greeted him.

"Bom," was the reply. The surfer kept staring out at the huge waves and the pros who were ripping it up quite far out.

Paco stuck with Portuguese. "Do you have any boards we can use?"

The request drew a quizzical gaze. "*You* surfers?"

Paco enthusiastically replied "Sim!" *Yes*! He nodded to another guy drinking a caiparinha, Brazil's national cocktail, on the far side of the hut and said something I couldn't catch. This guy gestured to us to follow him. We three trekked across the road to a locked hut where they stored a myriad of boards. We guessed that these belonged to people who only came out to surf on the weekends or in good weather. Today nobody was here except the pros.

"Which boards do you want?"

We grabbed two, gave the fellow a few reais and headed for the surf. A gust of wind grabbed the edge of my board and almost ripped it from my arms. I pushed into the wind and strode down the beach beside Paco. Once we reached a group of guys surfing, he stopped and pointed at them, yelling to me, "I'm going over there."

I took one look out at what was in front of them and yelled back, "I'm going to stay in the middle instead!" As soon as Paco left, I began doubting the wisdom of my choices.

> *OMG! What* **am** *I doing here? I'm not a pro...and these conditions are pretty extreme.*

But I had got myself this far and felt compelled to paddle out.

So I jumped on my board and started moving away from the beach. Fifty feet out the waves were breaking over me. I made it through the first few sets. The farther out I got, the larger the waves got. I adapted to avoid getting pulled under. When I saw a wave coming, I would roll my board over and pull the nose down so it could not wipe me out. Popping out on the other side, I'd break the surface, then flip my board back over, get back on, paddle a few strokes before having to repeat the whole sequence. Roll over, pull down, go under, pop up again and breathe, paddle.

Occasionally a wave was too big and I would get thrown back into the wash and roll around like a piece of wet laundry. As soon as I could, I'd surface, grab a quick breath, roll the board, get back on and start attacking the waves with my arms. The salt water was hitting me in the face with such force that, in no time, my lungs were burning and water and snot were continually running from my nose. I felt as if I was drowning more than I was surfing.

Suddenly, I broke through. I had made it out past the beach break. Now only the occasional rogue wave would hit me and send me down into the depths, where I would get sucked under and not know which way was up.

And then I saw a giant wave rolling towards me, not quite yet broken. I yanked on the side of my board to turn it down the wave, paddled a few strokes and then I was up and on, streaking down the face of a nine-footer.

For a glorious few seconds.

Then I was falling head over heels, right down the face of the wave. Everything was in silent slow motion. And then I hit the water. The wave forced me down and down, submerged me deep in the belly of this giant washing machine. Time stopped.

My board was being tossed about like a cork in the wash. The leash that was connected to my board tugged at my ankle. I didn't know how deep I was or how long I had been under. All I knew is that I was almost out of breath.

Panic!

The next second, I broke the surface long enough to take a quick half-breath before being hit by another wave. Down and down, round and round I went.

> *So this is how I die....*

Blue in the face and almost completely out of breath, I broke the surface again and grabbed another half-breath before the next wave hit. Over and over again, I got sucked under, rolled around, tossed up, only to get sucked under again.

> *Forget drowning in my business. I am literally going to drown here.*

Somehow I was finally able to grab hold of the leash, pull my board toward me, get on top of it and use it like a boogie board to ride the next white wash of a wave back to shore.

Feeling the sand under my palms, I pushed forward and stood up, only to collapse again on the beach after taking three steps. In a daze, I vaguely heard voices yelling around me. Exhausted, I let myself be dragged up the beach in the driving rain by the surfer from the hut and the guy who rented us our boards. They propped me up in a chair under the shelter of the small stand. Someone laughed and said in Portuguese, "Buddy, only the *pros* are out today." A bottle of cachaça, Brazil's most popular drink, appeared in my hand. I took a swig and immediately spat most of it out on the ground. More laughter.

Lifting my head slowly, I caught sight of Paco walking up the beach. As he approached, I realized how close I had come to dying that day. And I also realized that I had felt never more alive than in those moments when I was wrestling with the waves. Perhaps Paco could see that in my eyes. He looked at me and said, "Pretty crazy out there, eh?" He then sat down beside me and took a big swig from my bottle. We both looked at each other and started laughing profusely.

That wasn't the last time I went surfing with Paco. In fact, we hit the waves every time we traveled to Latin America after that. The more times we went, the better I got at judging the weather and the waves, the better I got at learning how to manage situations where I could drown.

Surviving the surf with Paco - Grumari Bay, Brazil (2009)

Throw me in the deep end. And throw me in again. If I don't drown, I will keep learning and I'll keep getting stronger.

Good thing that's what I was coming to believe. Because on April 20th 2010 a new wave hit Aqua-Guard.

Rieko and I had just arrived home from Chicago a few days earlier. But something was happening in the Gulf of Mexico: the news was reporting a massive explosion and oil gushing from a deep well at the BP Deepwater Horizon platform. Eleven people killed and many missing. When I returned to the office, the phone was ringing off the hook with calls from all over the world. It wasn't until ten days later that we got all the facts.

The largest oil spill in U.S. history was unfolding in front of our eyes. Within a month, BP had given our company a large contract to manufacture and ship as many RBS TRITON oil skimming systems as we could to the Gulf. For Aqua-Guard, this was a huge opportunity. We hired ex-oil spill response people and based them in Louisiana to supervise the installation of our skimming systems on all types of vessels available to go offshore. And at the office in Vancouver, we ran around like chickens with our heads cut off for almost three months, trying to get as much equipment out the door as we could. We had all hands on deck. Even our two boys Dylan and Devon were helping assemble and ship equipment at night and on weekends.

At the same time, my father was arrested for suspicion of anti-trust activities—yet again. I was dealing with negotiations regarding Vikoma's acquisition of Aqua-Guard. LP was pushing me to get the sale of the business done. And in the midst of all of this, the date of our Amazon journey kept getting closer and closer.

I was being pulled in so many directions that I felt like I was drowning (yet again!). But all my work with coach Kevin and that experience of almost drowning with Paco—literally—in Brazil helped me move through this current chaos and manage greater amounts of stress. I seemed better able to move through decisions quicker, get a lot done faster and deal effectively with all that was going on. Of course, the easy way out would be to step into the eye of the current storm and sell the company. That, I believed, would get me the freedom I had always dreamed of.

Yet, I was torn.

Lynne Twist had had a profound effect on me. Even though I began making up excuses in my head *not* to go to South America with my family, for reasons I couldn't explain, no matter how crazy things got at work, I was drawn again and again to the Amazon and felt compelled to make the trip happen. I couldn't put a finger on exactly why, but I had a strong sense I needed to go. So I spoke to our team. They were running hard, but agreed we had all the right people in the right seats. And Cam had the ability to run the company without me for a few weeks while I would be unreachable deep in the jungle.

When late July rolled around, the BP Horizon spill was still in full "go" mode. Vikoma was breathing down our necks to finish the deal to sell. There was just one thing holding me back from signing.

The Amazon.

CHAPTER 11
Awakening the Dreamer

Nestled in a valley between active volcanoes a mere 9,350 feet above sea level lies Quito, the capital of Ecuador. As our plane approached the old city in darkness, I could see lights along the strip of a runway. The pilot's voice came over the crackle of the intercom, mumbling something in Spanish about preparing to land. Diverting my focus away from the everyday, I ran through my usual standard mental cross-check: we had all our carry-ons with us, and as long as our few checked items had been transferred safely through Houston's George W. Bush airport, we would have all the gear we needed in the Amazon. Long-sleeved, lightweight shirts and pants to keep the mosquitoes away and lower our risk of contracting malaria. Kayak bags to keep our gear dry when transferring from canoes to shore. Unlike most of the climbing or ski adventures of the past, for this journey we wouldn't require any more special technical equipment than this. We would soon find out that, most of all, we would need open minds.

With a bump, we landed. Tired and excited, all five Bennetts loaded onto an old bus to get shuttled from the aircraft to the arrivals area. As soon as we emerged from customs, we grabbed our gear from the airline conveyor belt and began pushing our way through the crowd. The locals, waiting for friends and relatives to arrive, were slow to move from their spots to make way for us. A throng of taxi drivers, anxious for our fare, were trying to help us get through from the other side of the crowd. Swimming through this maelstrom of people was daunting, but we pushed through to a recognized taxi stand.

"Café Cultura, Avenida Robles y Reina Victoria," I told the driver, as we climbed into the cab. I had no idea how to get to the small boutique hotel in central Quito and the streets around us were pitch black. That knot I had felt in my stomach when I had taken my family across the border into Mexico was back again. This time, the question rumbling around in my head was different.

*What has **really** brought us here?*

After about forty minutes of winding our way through the city, we finally arrived at our destination. One of the family members who owned the establishment had stayed up to greet us. Carrying our complimentary cold beer for us, they led the way up the stairs to our rooms.

Every step we took, no matter how lightly we walked, made the floorboards squeak. That made me glad we were climbing to the top floor, where we might stand a chance of not being woken by other travelers. One by one, we took a well-deserved shower and then climbed into bed to crash for the night.

We all should have slept like babies. But the high altitude was already having an effect. Pounding heads made us all restless that night. Breakfast the next morning was a groggy blur. Thankfully the plan was to stay another two days in Quito to get acclimatized before Lynne Twist, our guides and the rest of our group would join us. Then our journey through the Andes Valley of the Volcanoes down into the Amazon could begin.

Over the next two days, Rieko and the kids and I explored Quito's beautiful cobblestone streets and parks in the mornings. We would return from the hustle and bustle of the city to Café Cultura in the afternoon. There we would sit in the courtyard behind the hotel's iconic big wrought iron gate, playing cards quietly and watching the trees and flowers gracefully wind their way along the wall. It was while we were here, late in the second afternoon, that we heard a mini-bus rumble up outside the gate. Through the iron bars, we could see Lynne, her assistant Sara and a few of our soon-to-be group of twelve hop out. A warm welcome, hugs all around and an agreement to meet for dinner and a briefing at 6 p.m. Little did we strangers know what we would encounter together and how close we would all become.

Dinner was over and we had settled back, wine glasses in hand, for our briefing. I was taken once again by Lynne's passion and knowledge. From her seat at the head of the table, she told us more about the Pachamama Alliance and what they had been doing together with the Achuar since 1995.

From 1964 to 1992, Ecuador's northern pristine rainforest had been desecrated by the Texas oil company Texaco. Chevron acquired Texaco in 2001. Ten years later, an Ecuadorian court found Chevron to be guilty of environmental negligence and issued the company an $8 billion fine, the largest environmental penalty ever awarded. That fine is still in contention today. Even so, Big Oil has continued to make a large push to develop many other areas of the Ecuadorian Amazon, Yasuní National Park, one of the most biologically diverse areas on the planet, being one of them.

Meanwhile, Rafael Vicente Correa Delgado, the populist president of Ecuador, had invited the international community to help protect the Amazon. Knowing that his country was very poor and in need of income, he believed the only way to stop selling the resources under the Amazon was to get other countries to band together and chip in US $3.6 billion to pay for the value of the oil in the ground. If they could do this quickly, then the Amazon could be protected for all time. This would prove to be a great challenge for President Correa.

Through all this, the Pachamama Alliance had been working with the Achuar and Shuar tribes to keep the big oil companies at bay. Lynne introduced Daniel, the tall Eucadorian gentleman who had joined us after dinner, as the fourth co-founder of the Alliance. A local guide and good friend of both John Perkins and the Twists, he had built the Kapawi Lodge, the ecolodge we would be staying at deep in the Amazon rainforest. Daniel Koupermann and the Pachamama Alliance had built the lodge with the blessings of the Achuar people. Their mission was to bring a limited number of visitors from the modern world close enough so they could visit and learn directly from the Achuar. Kapawi Lodge would be a staging ground for our journeys deeper into the Amazon.

By the next morning, we were all feeling a lot better. It was easy for all five of us to lift our bags onto the top of the small mini-bus and strap them to the roof. This sixteen-passenger vehicle would be our transport as we meandered through the Valley of the Volcanoes, past massive Mount Cotopaxi which had been seismically active as recently as 2002, on our way to the small town of Baños where we would stay the night. We were booked into a small hotel, precariously perched on the side of an active volcano called Tungurahua ("Throat of Fire").

Once we were all settled into our rooms above Baños, Dylan, Devon, Daniel and I decided to hike down the mountain to the main town. It was a Saturday afternoon and the local market was bustling. We saw live guinea pigs in cages. Hanging from hooks above them were several carcasses that had been cooked on an open flame. Daniel saw our faces and laughed. At his invitation to try some, we gingerly asked a shop owner if we could sample a piece. He obligingly pulled some blistered flesh off with his bare fingers and passed it to each of us. The meat was surprisingly chewy. We learned that guinea pigs, a staple in both Ecuador and Peru, were a low-impact alternative to costly cattle.

We ambled through the village for another 45 minutes and then suddenly Dylan doubled over. Holding his stomach, he looked up at me and I said, "I'm not feeling well. I have to get back up the hill to the hotel." Daniel called for the mini-bus to come to pick us up. We boarded, took our seats and let the vehicle do the steep climb back up the mountain for us. Dylan looked greener and greener with every switchback. The instant we arrived outside his bungalow, he ran from the bus, threw up on the ground and then disappeared inside the bathroom.

As soon as Dylan ran for the bungalow, I started to feel awful too. Dylan was huddled around the toilet on the cool bathroom floor. I asked him to move over as I vomited into it. For the next twelve hours, we both lay on that deliciously cool floor, sharing the same white basin and playing tag team vomit.

By Sunday morning, we were able to crawl to our beds. We slept until noon and woke up just in time to be picked up by a taxi driver who was supposed to take us to our group. The plan was that they would leave the hotel and take our luggage with them and go to do some rappelling down a waterfall somewhere outside of town, after which we would meet up and continue together on our journey.

At noon, Dylan and I stumbled out of our room and grabbed the taxi that was waiting for us outside our bungalow, as pre-arranged. It ended up being a random driver who happened to be there, not the one we were supposed to go with. He had no idea where to take us to meet up with our group, so I had the driver drop us off in the town center next to a large church. I must have got my wires crossed because that wasn't our pick-up point. Still somewhat weak from our tag team ordeal, we sat on a bench for a couple of hours, watching people pass by and wondering where our group was. We didn't have a cell phone with us, so we had no way of making contact.

Little did we know Daniel had found out we had taken the wrong taxi and been looking for us for quite some time. I decided to leave Dylan watching a couple of locals play backgammon and a Canadian couple playing cribbage while I checked out the church. Immediately, the back of the head of a tall man towering over the crowd in the sanctuary caught my eye. "Daniel!", I called out. To this day, I still don't know what drew us both to go inside the church at the same time.

Daniel brought us to the rest of our group and we all boarded our mini-bus. Leaving the relative calm of the town center, we made our bumpy way down from the Valley of the Volcanoes towards the edge of the Amazon and the region's small capital of Puyo and, from there, towards a town called Shell (named after the oil company). Just before we arrived in Shell, a massive nine-foot snake slithered out in front of our bus.

Was this a sign of things to come?

Shell's most distinguishing feature was the fact that its small landing strip sits at the edge of the Amazon rainforest. There, parked on the runway when we arrived, were a couple of small, piston-powered Cessnas. A 60-minute flight would take us deep into the Amazon. Deep into Achuar territory.

As we began hauling our gear toward the planes, Daniel caught my attention. "Do you want to split your family into the two planes?", he asked. "Why?", I returned innocently. "Just for safety's sake...*if you know what I mean*?", he whispered. "Oh." I thought for a second and then turned to Rieko to ask her opinion. She replied out loud, "We all go *together*. If we go down, we all go together." We were agreed.

One by one, each person in the group had to stand on a scale to be weighed. Then their bag had to be weighed. Then the weight of all of us, plus our bags, was tallied to make sure that the way we were distributing everyone and everything would not overload either Cessna.

Once that important detail was taken care of and our bags were loaded, I opened the co-pilot door to our plane and pulled myself up. I looked at the pilot and, seeing his face paint, realized he was an Achuar tribal member. He probably only spoke Spanish and Achuar. As Rieko and the kids loaded into the rear of the plane, I tried speaking to him in my broken Spanish. I could hear Dylan commenting from the back that he saw a guy standing beside the plane with a tiny fire extinguisher. Laughing, he asked us all, "Now what is he going to do with that?"

As we taxied along, I was intensely aware of how very short the runway was. We quickly picked up speed...and then we were airborne. A steep ascent and in seconds we could see the runway below us, lined with green banana trees. Beyond this facade, in all directions, the rainforest had been stripped. We gained more height and more perspective. The land below us looked like it had been raped. Everywhere was a criss-crossing of oil pipes and dirt access roads. The land itself looked scorched and black. The pools of black oil and the destruction of the natural world reminded me of flying over the Sinai in Egypt all those years ago.

Nothing has changed in the last three decades....

Lost in my thoughts, I lost track of time.

Gradually, as we flew further and further away from civilization, the environmental degradation slowed. As we crossed a river, the pilot pointed below us and said, "Achuar". We were now in their territory, an area protected, for now, from the oil industry. I was all too aware in that moment that President Correa still needed vast international funds to truly protect it.

For the rest of the flight, we all stared out at the unspoiled rainforest. As far as the eye could see lay a thick canopy of green and yellow, a carpet of treetops through which flowed virgin rivers. Fed by the high Andes Mountains, these tributaries converged to form the headwaters of the mighty Amazon that flows from Ecuador through Peru to Brazil on its way to the Atlantic Ocean almost 4,350 miles away.

There were no signs of industry anywhere. The area was as pristine as it had been for tens of thousands of years. This land was untouched by our modern world.

I had never seen anything like this in my life, not even in Canada. Below us were the lungs of the world, breathing.

I looked over my shoulder to see Rieko and the kids staring in awe out the side windows. They were silent for the entire flight as they took in the vista below.

To our right, we could see thatched roofs and a few huts. An Achuar village in the midst of all this natural beauty, right beside the large Pastaza River, a tributary of the mighty Amazon. People coming out from under the forest canopy, looking up at us and waving. A dirt runway marked in the ground by two lines of yellow flowers.

Lynne and our new friends in the other Cessna pulled ahead of us and started their descent. We followed them, dropping slowly, at a distance of about a thousand yards. Their wheels hit the dirt runway with a poof of dust. Then it was our turn. The green of the rainforest whizzed by our window as we came in to land. And then a sudden thud as we made contact with the earth. We were suddenly forced forward in our seats and could feel the tight tug of the seat belts across our chests as the wheels of the plane grabbed the brown soil. The green blur outside the window became a clear picture: trees everywhere in so many hues it was impossible to fathom so many shades of one color actually existed. The tops of some of them had yellow blooms (I found out later they were mighty kapok trees). We came to a full stop in this magical scene.

Right in front of me, thirty feet away, were the headwaters of the mighty Amazon.

This is where it all begins.

The pilot gave me the thumbs up signal, smiled and said, "Bienvienido a Amazonas!" (Welcome to the Amazon!). I turned around in my seat to catch sight of Rieko and the kids with mile-wide smiles on their faces. We were going to spend the next ten days fully immersed in this. Grabbing the latch to the plane's door, I opened it for us all and was the first to step out into the center of the natural world.

Tribal members with the same yellow, black and red headdresses Lynne had envisioned years before were emerging from the jungle. In a flash, some of Lynne's words from her Gathering of Titans presentation in Boston, words that I had forgotten until now, came back to me.

> "*The intent of the Pachamama Alliance is to empower the indigenous peoples of the Amazon who are its natural custodians. During our first meeting with the Achuar, they were very direct in telling us that* **if we were coming to help them**, *then we shouldn't waste our time. But* **if we were coming because we knew that our liberation is bound to theirs**, *then we could work together to change the dream of the modern world.*"

The people in front of us were the same people who had said those words. And we were now some of the few from the modern world being allowed to experience the world in its natural state with them, to learn and understand their way of life. Some of the few being asked to return to our daily lives and share our experiences with friends and strangers and enroll people in protecting Pachamama.

The Achuar hope that, by doing so, we will "awaken" people from the dream of the modern world, the materialistic illusion so many live with that money, status and power are all important. Once awakened, people can see what is

Kapawi Ecolodge - Ecuador (2010)

Our Achuar guide

really important—the natural world, family and our unending connection to Pachamama—and that the modern world cannot exist without the natural world. Once awakened, we can choose a path to freedom that will lead to survival for all of us, rather than blindly follow along the one we are currently on. The path that puts our very future as a species at risk.

Guides and two canoes fitted with small engines were waiting for us at the riverbank. We loaded our waterproof bags in before taking our seats, eight to a canoe. The sound of the rushing river lapping against the sides of our canoes was somehow calming. Pink Amazon River dolphins played under the mangroves as we hummed along the last leg of our journey to the Kapawi Lodge.

Hundreds of miles away from civilization, we were grateful to eventually arrive at the lodge's small dock. Achuar tribal members who were caretakers of the Kapawi greeted us, including Tinchu, who would be one of our guides for the next week or so. As we walked across the creaky dock to our cabanas, I wondered how many crocodiles were looking at us from the murky waters of the lagoon around us.

Did the Universe really bring us to this place? And if so, why?

I found no answers in the faces or in the trees around me.

It must have been really difficult to get any building materials this far into the jungle. Daniel had done an amazing job working with the Achuar. Each cabana sat on stilts over the lagoon. The humble rooms were very rustic, open to the air and with no running water. A couple of hammocks hung above each large outdoor deck. Large mosquito nets draped over the beds. To heat water for showering, the "staff" would place thick plastic bags on the boardwalk in the sun each morning. The technology was simple: we would grab a bag, hang it up in our shower and turn a small valve to let the warm water flow through our shower head. The food we ate would be all locally sourced. Anything from the "outside" world had to be flown in, so the selection of modern world items would be pretty thin.

The Amazon rainforest was nothing like I had imagined. We were on the equator in August: the temperature was in the mid-70s with some humidity, but not too much. This was a perfect climate for humans. We were prepared for masses of mosquitoes, but there were very few. It seemed like everything here was in perfect balance.

On the equator, it gets dark at 6 p.m. every night of the year. As the sun started to set over the lagoon, the noise of the animals in the jungle rose louder and louder until we could barely hear ourselves talk. The deafening buzz of encroaching night had a rhythm all its own, almost as if the rainforest was a well-tuned orchestra.

At 7:00 p.m., we all met with Lynne and Daniel for a briefing on what the next week would bring. Apparently, we were to visit an Achuar village a couple of times and also take part in an overnight ceremony there led by two shaman. Before we went, we would have to fast for twenty-four hours to prepare our bodies for a tonic, a hallucinogenic called ayahuasca, which would cause spiritual revelations. We didn't really know what this was, but it sounded interesting.

True to their word, the Achuar brought us to one of their villages on the Pastaza the next day. The village elders guided us to sit in the dirt on several small stumps under a large, open-air style thatched roof. There we were greeted by the village chief and asked to drink a small bowl of chicha. Several of the chief's wives had prepared this drink from manioc root by boiling it overnight, then chewing it and spitting the residue back into a pot over and over again until it finally formed the milky substance we were to down. Chicha is the only liquid the Achuar drink. I took one sip and choked it down. My son Devon, sitting beside me, drank the entire bowl in one gulp. He looked up at me as if to say, "Ha! Mine is all gone, and you still have most in your bowl." The instant the village women saw that Devon's bowl was empty, they came to fill it back up. I looked over at Devon and gave him a smirk.

That afternoon, the soccer ball we had brought with us came out of hiding. In a few minutes, our kids were playing a match with the youth of the village in an open patch of dirt. By the end, everyone was covered in red dust.

Over the next few nights, Daniel took our kids out in a canoe to fish and view the billions of stars in the pitch black sky. We were deep in the Amazon rainforest and as a family were witnessing things together that only a few from the outside world had seen.

One morning we were told it was time to prepare for our ceremony. That meant nothing to eat until the next day. It also meant a journey deeper into the jungle.

We traveled upriver a few miles in canoes, then beached them on the muddy riverbank. Here began our three-hour hike through the jungle with Tinchu, our Achuar guide.

After about ninety minutes, Tinchu had us stop for a half-hour meditation in the jungle. We each sat alone and listened to the sounds of the world around us. I closed my eyes to listen. My ears seemed to become hyper-sensitive within a few minutes: I could hear even the smallest creature, whether they were moving on the rainforest floor or high up in the canopy. Then a loud clap of thunder rumbled far off in the distance. Those thirty minutes seemed to last ages. Tinchu eventually reappeared in front of me, leading everyone single file through the undergrowth and clearing the way with his machete.

The thunder kept getting closer and closer until, at one point, the heavens just opened. The rain literally poured down like a waterfall. We had no choice but to trudge through it. A small creek we had to cross had quickly become a raging river. Our only way forward was to inch our way across a fallen 15-foot log above the tumultuous waters. We formed a careful line, balancing on the log, ready to help each person make their way along the slippery surface until they got close to the other side, where we all had to jump down to the shore.

Safely on the far side, we trudged through the mud for what seemed like forever. To our eyes, there was no trail, no signs to give anyone a sense of direction. We were relying entirely on the judgment of our Achuar tribesmen not to get us too lost.

The rain finally slowed. We could tell the late afternoon sun was coming out again because we had arrived at a large opening in the jungle where it was possible to hike along the side of the river. Far ahead, we could see a few roofs of thatched palm leaves. We had made it to the village! Soaking wet and covered in mud, we arrived in time to see our canoes coming alongside with Kina and a welcome change of clothes. Everyone was in surprisingly good spirits, considering we had had nothing to eat since the night before. Now that we were here, it was time to prepare for the evening's ceremony.

As a family, we had agreed that we would all take part in the evening's event. Devon, fourteen, and Dylan, sixteen, would take the ayahuasca, even though that was a bit scary for us as parents. Kina, who was only ten at the time, would not.

At one end of the village stood a large hut without any walls. Just four pillars held up the thatched roof. We were invited to each lay a banana leaf outside on the ground and to wait. I lay mine under a banana tree. Apparently, our group would be here under the stars most of the night.

Dylan being painted by the Achuar

Lynne Twist & Sara Vetter with Achuar children

Rieko deep in the Amazon

Villagers high in the Andes

Around 7:30, two shamans appeared on the scene. They each lit a fire about 50 yards apart. We broke into two groups of six and sat in a tight semi-circle around each shaman and his fire. Our shaman prepared a tonic made of two vines called ayahuasca. He put the spiritual medicine into a bowl, took a few mouthfuls and spat them back into the bowl to mix the tonic. He then chanted for several minutes in the Achuar language before pouring an exact measure of the tonic into each of our smaller bowls. We worked our way around the circle, each individual taking a few gulps of the tonic from our own bowl. Then it was my turn. Dylan and Devon peered intently at me, as if to check with me one last time that I was okay with this before they took their portions.

Once we all had our share, the shaman chanted and whistled. Then Daniel told us it would be about forty minutes before the ayahuasca would begin to take effect. So we all stood up and went for a walk around the tiny village for half an hour, returning in time to lay on our individual banana leaves in the dirt. This would be our spot for the evening. As we lay on our backs, we were told that most of us would become violently sick and vomit for quite some time. We might even soil ourselves. Fortunately, we had Kina, Daniel and friend Sara there to look after us.

As I looked up into the sky and stars, the night seemed to become even darker. The palm and banana tree branches were waving gently in the wind. Over time, the banana leaves began to pulse red, yellow and blue to the rhythm of the crickets. The noise of the jungle was overpowering: it was as if someone had cranked the volume up on the stereo past eleven.

The pulsing colors and the loud sounds started making me feel awful. It was like a crazy circus ride.

I want to get off.

The intensity grew and grew. I felt totally out of control and worse by the minute. And then I rolled over and started retching violently, over and over again. It was terrible. Worse even than anything I had been through before.

Daniel came over, touched me on the shoulder and asked me if I was okay. The sound of his voice settled me down a bit. Strangely, after purging myself, I felt very calm. I heard him ask, "Are you with the plant?" I assumed so and weakly said, "Yes...yes...."

Daniel lifted me up, walked me to a spot and sat me down on something. I could vaguely see a shaman sitting on a log across from me. I stared at him, my body paralyzed. Then he started whistling and the sound began echoing through my brain. He had a fan-like object made of young palm leaves in his hand, which he started to wave in a circular motion. He drew a large breath of smoke into his mouth from a pipe and then blew the smoke directly at me, at the same time still whirling the fan in a circular motion, which made the smoke dance in strange ways towards me.

Suddenly the whirling fan morphed into a round sort of calendar...perhaps Mayan? In the center of the calendar was a face, the face of a man. Or was it more like the smiling face of Buddha? I squinted again and again. I could not believe what I was seeing. The face was clearly smiling at me and watching it gave me a warm, comforting feeling. The smile morphed into a serious stare, which at first scared me. Then I understood. The face was trying to tell me something without speaking. I sat back and took in a feeling, a sense of being given a great responsibility. Then the serious look turned back into a smile and that warm feeling filled my body again.

Daniel helped me up, steadied me and led me back to my banana leaf. Lying back down, face to the heavens, I found myself looking up at a billion stars through the jungle canopy. I lay there, content. I could feel a wind picking up behind me and the trees started moving back and forth with each of my breaths. A large gust of wind swept through the jungle and suddenly I was airborne, flying up, up and over the village and the rainforest. It was as if I had become a very large bird like a condor. I flew over the Amazon. Below me, a man paddled a canoe up the river. Then I became that man calmly paddling. I could hear children laughing on the shore and see more children playing near the water. A man was fishing several yards away from them on the shore. I became the man fishing and suddenly heard all the children playing behind me. Some of the children ran over to me and touched me as if they knew me. I could understand their language fluently. They were calling me "father" and "uncle". Although I was very confused, I felt warm and loved. Without warning, I then became the large bird again, flying high over the rainforest and looking down on the green trees with yellow tops.

Someone was crying. I was back on my banana leaf, coherent and able to get up and walk over to find a mosquito net, which I climbed under before falling asleep.

I awoke the next morning to the sound of chatter from the villagers. Time had no meaning for me when I awoke.

How long had I been flying over the rainforest? Did I sleep at all?

It didn't really matter.

That next day, Lynne and Daniel told us that our visions would most likely mean nothing to us right now, but as time passes they will take on more and more meaning. Daniel saw how important understanding mine was to me and so he asked the shaman to interpret a part of my dream for me. "From the wind and the canoe, you will travel to areas where most people do not go and you will go against the status quo..." was his reply. Over time, my vision of the man fishing and the Mayan calendar has gotten stronger. It is somehow deeply rooted in my consciousness.

I have since learned that the condor is part of an ancient Andean prophecy. It is said that around 2012, when the last few years of a 500-year cycle of their calendar ends and a new cycle begins, there will be great change within both the modern and the natural worlds. During this time, there will be a major disruption and a transformation. The eagle, which represents the "modern world" and its technology, will be forced to fly together in the sky with the condor, which represents the "natural world" and its jungles, oceans, rivers and earth. That is to say, both worlds will have to work together as equals to protect Pachamama. If this does not happen, the prophecy says, then Pachamama will flick us off like a flea and start again.

August 12th 2010. The twenty-first anniversary of Rieko's and my wedding. Back at the Kapawi Lodge, I hooked up a plastic bag in my outdoor shower and opened the valve. Just as the ceremony had cleansed my mind of confusion, the warm water cleansed my body of the red soil that covered me from head to toe.

In the afternoon, Daniel asked if anyone wanted to go for a swim down the river. At first, I was scared. As parents, we assumed that, since this was the Amazon, there must be piranhas and other dangerous things lurking beneath the surface. The children had seen many caimans and six-foot-long river otters on their nighttime fishing escapades with Daniel. We had heard that a large anaconda had been sighted in the area.

But Daniel and our guide Tinchu both agreed that where they were going to take us was safe at the moment: they had scouted it out. If they'd asked us a week earlier, there would have been no way we would have even considered jumping into the Amazon. But much had changed in just a few days. Rieko and I agreed the family would go swimming: we trusted that Daniel, Tinchu and the rainforest would keep us safe.

The seven of us boarded a few rafts and slowly started drifting down the river. Dylan, usually nervous of entering murky waters, was the first to jump in, quickly followed by Kina. Devon, usually the most daring one, was last to slip off the raft into the Amazon's coolness. Once the whole family was in, we linked arms and let ourselves be slowly carried along by the river's currents. The huge grins on our faces said it all: we didn't need to speak and we didn't for a full forty minutes. We just held on to each other, floating gently and peacefully along, drifting free of any thoughts of the past or the future, unafraid of any dangers that might lurk below or above. I think we bonded more as a family in those forty minutes than we did in any other experience we've had together before or since.

The next day the weather was a bit sketchy. Flying back to Shell could be hit or miss. Our pilot decided to give it a try anyway, so we said "so long" to our new-found friends, the Achuar, the true custodians of the Amazon rainforest. As we stood beside our two planes, the elders gave our translators a message for us.

"You have learned of our people and our ways and how important it is to protect the natural world. Now you understand why the modern and natural worlds must co-exist and learn from each other. But first you must help to change the dream of your modern world."

As the engine of the Cessna started to roar, I looked back to see the yellow, black and red headdresses slowly disappearing back into the rainforest. We careened down the dirt runway, the flowers lining the sides of the runway turning into a yellow blur. Then we were up, banking over the village where we had spent our last night. The pristine canopy of the forest was exactly the same as when we had arrived. But what we saw when we looked at it was different.

We had been changed by our experience of the natural world with the Achuar. The dreamer had awakened in all of us. We had seen through the illusion of our modern world, the illusion that pitted people against Nature.

We gradually made our way back to our modern lives one experience at a time. First, a bumpy flight to Shell, then a drive back through Puyo and on to Otavalo, a small Ecuadorean village high in the Andes. We spent a few days here, visiting with local Andean mountain tribes and working in the fields with them.

Late one afternoon, we met with two local shamans. Rieko and the other ladies went with Maria Juana, a female shaman, into a mud hut. There they underwent a ceremony, which we found out later was similar, but not quite as intense, as what we did. Afterwards, Maria did individual healing practices for each of the women, specific to whatever was going on in their bodies. For her specific healing, Rieko was stripped naked and then lifted up by the ankles and shaken by Maria Juana's son. After that, the shaman read Rieko's life energy. Speaking through a translator, Maria Juana said that Rieko was generally healthy, centered and a calm spirit, that she had a strong, calm heart, that she carried kindness and would have a good life. Kina, being too young for a reading, would have to wait for a few years before she could have hers.

Meanwhile, Daniel, Devon, Dylan and I had gone with a male shaman into a cold, damp concrete hut with a dirt floor. There, at the shaman's request, we Bennett boys stripped down to our underwear and stepped into the middle of the room. What happened next involved dirt, a volcanic stone, stinging nettles, candles, a match and alcohol. Needless to say, it was uncomfortable. Before the ritual cleansing and chanting, we were each given a candle and instructed to rub it all over our bodies. Once cleansed, the shaman lit the candles and examined them to read our "life flame".

Daniel translated from Kichwa for us.

"Dylan will have no trouble with school: he is a hard worker and will do very well in life and will help Pachamama and someday be someone very important. Devon will be all over the place, but when he finds what he really loves (which will happen at a young age), he will excel and be quite famous for it. Nigel...your mission in life is to protect Pachamama, our Mother Earth."

Kina, Rieko, Nigel, Dylan and Devon

We are all busy in our businesses and our daily routines. There are always excuses not to leave work for more than a few days, not to travel for adventure or experience life with our family. If I had listened to that little voice in my head that played the non-stop guilt tape about leaving the office, I would have stayed in my safe zone and we never would have gone on this amazing journey. But my gut had told me to go, and I had trusted there would be something important out there for us to discover. And my gut was right. This journey was much more than just an adventure: it not only had a huge impact on my family. It helped me find my purpose.

We all returned to Quito totally changed, totally awake to the natural world. This Amazon experience "awoke the dreamer" in all of us. It connected us very deeply to ourselves, to each other and to Pachamama and made us start to question what really is most important in life.

For me, that meant getting very clear that success is not about acquiring money, fame, fortune or popularity. It's not about any of the things popular culture teaches us we need to be happy: the Armani and the Gucci, the Maserati and the Ferrari. It's not the 'I's we should pay attention to. It's the 'A's like the teachings of yoga and the Dalai Lama, the wisdom of Pachamama (Mother Earth) and philia (brotherly love). A life well lived is about love and community. It's about loving the people you live with and those you work with. And it is about loving Pachamama and helping protect her for future generations.

CHAPTER 12
The Eagle & the Condor

My head was spinning as our plane approached Vancouver. The experiences we had just had as a family with new friends shook me at a deeper level than anything I had ever experienced before. It brought my personal "why" into focus and opened me up to my greater purpose. I wasn't just here to father a business and a family. I was here to protect Pachamama. That solidified my business "why" and made everything that Simon Sinek had said at that Gathering of Titans session back in 2009 even more poignant.

With a bump, we hit the tarmac at YVR airport. We were back in the modern world, the world of the Eagle. And I was coming home to complete the sale of Aqua-Guard to a U.K. firm that would fold it into their company.

When I arrived back in the office, the first thing I noticed were signs that our hunch had been correct: offshore was the new frontier for oil production. And we had wisely chosen to make that our sweet spot at just the right time.

As things began calming down from the BP Deepwater Horizon spill, the universe started to open up to us. By late 2010, we were starting to get calls from clients all over the world. First it was Petrobras in Brazil. Then the Korean Coast Guard. Then the Petroleum Association of Japan and PDVSA, Venezuela's state-owned oil and gas company. Then a multitude of offshore ship supply contractors working for all these companies. Deepwater Horizon had hit them all like a ton of bricks. What had happened to BP could have happened to any of the major global oil companies or to any one of their supply contractors.

Suddenly, everyone was waking up to the reality that they were simply not prepared to handle an oil spill of this magnitude offshore. Proposals we had submitted to clients over the years got pulled off the back burner. And then the purchase orders started showing up, first one at a time, then two at a time, and then three or more together. From 2011 to 2016, we could barely keep up with the demand for our large offshore URO machines. We were non-stop busy building and installing them all over the world.

We were flying. The risk we had taken to push into areas where we perceived a need, a niche and high margins had paid off.

But we had agreed to sell the company long before any of this had started to happen. And I was just awakening to the full scope of Aqua-Guard's "why".

My family and I had experienced and learned so much in such a short period of time in Ecuador. We had seen first-hand the untouched pristine territory of the Achuar people. We had witnessed the ever-expanding deforestation and contamination of our planet in towns like Shell, reminiscent of what I had seen so many years ago along the Gulf of Suez.

I had realized that we were living in a dream, the dream of the modern world. The concept of hoarding money and material things had been programmed into all of us at a young age. Raise your kids to go to the best schools so they can make the most money and gain the highest prestige for the family. Show that off by hoarding the largest homes, the fanciest cars, the fastest boats, the most exclusive summer homes. On and on it went. We were all living the dream.

But my eyes were open now. The dream of our modern world was pulling us all in the wrong direction. I could see what the Andeans and other indigenous peoples had been predicting for thousands of years: the need for balance between our modern world and its technology and the natural world and its wisdom.

Greed and hoarding push our race to do crazy things. They push us to destroy thousands of acres of rainforest in the name of progress. They push us to pollute our oceans and rivers all over the planet in the name of growth. They push us to only consider the short-term gain. An underlying mindset of scarcity compels us to pile up as many material goods in our corner as possible, no matter what the costs are to our planet and our society.

We need to be moving in the opposite direction to find that balance between technology and wisdom and to, like the peoples of the Amazon and the Andes said, have the Eagle fly with the Condor.

We live on an abundant planet. And, just like the Achuar are the true stewards of the rainforest, we are this world's natural caretakers. We must consider the ramifications of everything we do for at least seven generations ahead of us. We must take care of this world for them.

We especially must protect regions of our planet that house precious indigenous wisdom about Nature. The regions where plants grow that yield medicines like none other on Earth. The rainforests that truly are the lungs of the planet, filtering out contaminants, eating up the carbon dioxide that causes global warming and creating oxygen for all life forms to breathe. The forests that create weather systems for rainclouds to form and drop the water essential for the planet's flora and fauna. For all species to survive, the ancient teachings tied to these places must be passed down.

My head was spinning with this new awareness. Awareness that left me in a quandary about what to do with our company.

Aqua-Guard's reason for existing was not just to design and provide the best oil spill response equipment on the planet. Although this was still important, our "Big Hairy Audacious Goal", as Verne Harnish would call it, was to "protect the world's most precious resource". That resource was water!

And here I was about to give up my platform, a network of contacts that stretched around the globe, my extensive business experience. All for a bag of cash? If I did, I would become one of the things I was most scared of becoming: a businessman who chose to cash out, who chose to have that liquidation event and then live ever after in "protection mode". After all, I would have to protect my pile of hard-earned cash for my family. I'd be creating, at least in my mind, a world of scarcity for my wife and children and myself.

This choice kicked up an internal struggle unlike anything I'd wrestled with yet. The entire deal was done. Yet I fell back into thinking about what was important, what was meaningful to me.

We had a good company. It provided everything our employees needed. It provided everything my family needed. And it also provided the world with solutions for protecting our global waterways.

And then the little voice in my head really got loud.

> *Cashing out will give me all the freedom I have always dreamed of. I'll be able to do whatever I want, to travel when and where I want. But won't that eventually get boring? And what about my*

self-worth? Yes, I'll have a big bag of cash. But will I end up just selling t-shirts on the beach so I have a reason to get out of bed?

To sell or not to sell Aqua-Guard? I couldn't believe how difficult this choice was. I'd been through many mental and physical challenges, everything from escaping Egypt and breaking off from my father's company to epic adventures climbing mountains. But this decision was tearing me apart.

I needed to get away to clear my head. I needed time and space to process this monumental decision that would affect myself and my family for many years to come.

There was only one place I went to when I needed to clear my head and that was outdoors. I have always been able to do my best thinking and processing outside. Whether it was simply a late night walk when our kids were asleep or a mountain bike ride in the wilderness or a backcountry ski adventure, guaranteed, at some point, I would come back with a clear mind and a solution.

My buddy Mark had a cousin who flew for a helicopter company based out of Whistler. We and six other biking buddies had heard about a possible ride off the top of Goat Mountain near Squamish. So Mark arranged for us all to be picked up by helicopter in the small town of Britannia Beach.

On an early Sunday morning in the fall of 2010, we found ourselves waiting on an old tarmac pad for the dull roar of helicopter blades. Running out onto the helipad, we slipped under the humming chopper blades to sling our heavy downhill bikes alongside the landing skids. At our thumbs up, the pilot powered up the chopper and lifted off. As we headed for the mountain top, I looked down to see our bikes dangling 50 feet below us. The chopper pilot, in a couple of trips, was able to shuttle all eight of us to the snowy top of Goat Mountain. Once on the ground, we unhooked our bikes, only to find ourselves pushing through deep slushy snow for quite some time until we finally hit beautifully smooth granite rock.

In preparation for a several-hour technical rip down the mountain, we donned our full body armor and full face helmets for the steep downhill ride to Britannia Beach. After an hour of amazingly fluid riding, I heard a crack. Suddenly I was flying through the air over my handlebars. I landed and blood began pouring out of my mouth. I had bitten a chunk out of my tongue. I got up and turned around, only to see that the rear triangle of my frame had snapped. The welding that held the rear of the bike together was broken and the back wheel was jammed. Mark and I tried to repair it, but it was an impossible task.

I was miles from anywhere on the top of a mountain without a bike I could ride. I couldn't even push it. So here began my day-long hike. I had to physically carry my 45-pound bike over my shoulder down the mountain. From where we were, I figured the trek would take me about seven to eight hours. Most of the group rode off, but Mark and a couple of guys stayed reasonably close to me.

I quickly ran out of water. The weather was dry and so were the creek beds. I would find small puddles in the dry beds and lick damp rocks with my mangled tongue for moisture. I was shattered, but I had no choice. I had to make it out. I didn't think I was going to arrive anywhere near civilization before nightfall. But I kept going, finally breaking out of the woods onto a small local road where I was able to get a ride home.

My body was spent and my tongue had a chunk missing. But my mind was super clear.

And I felt *very* alive.

A few weeks later, I returned with our Aqua-Guard racing team to Whistler for a bike race. Everything was going fine until my final lap of the brutally strenuous course. At the top of the lap was a large set of stairs that I had to jump. I heard a "smack" when I landed, followed by a very loud hiss. I had a flat tire. With only one lap to go, I decided not to repair it but to run to the finish line, carrying my bike over my shoulder. After all, I had recently carried a heavier bike seven hours down a mountain. Another 30 minutes on a racecourse should be relatively easy.

I lifted my bike over my shoulder and started to run. I could hear cheering coming from the crowd of spectators lining the course. These onlookers were encouraging me. I became stronger and stronger as I lapped back around the course to arrive at the stairs where I had blown the tire. This time, I had to run up the stairs carrying my bike. I struggled and tripped, got up and scrambled to the top. Ahead of me stretched the last 100 yards of the course, lined with hundreds of people. They could see I had a flat tire and was carrying my bike. The cheering got louder and louder as I approached the finish line. I gave it all I had, pulling up hidden reserves of energy I hadn't even used on Goat Mountain. As I collapsed in an exhausted heap on the ground, I only had one thought in my mind:

If I can push through these challenges, why am I still having such a hard time deciding whether to sell my company or not?

I'd been molded to believe that being an entrepreneur is all about starting, building and eventually selling your company for a big bag of cash.

My journey to the Amazon and the Andes made me aware that this is a myth. It was certainly no longer my dream. Perhaps, in my heart, it never really was. Everything I had been learning and experiencing since I left school all those years ago had brought me to this moment.

I just couldn't do it—I couldn't sell!

What if I take the company off the table? What if I keep the company and use the platform I've built over the past 30 years and leverage it to change the world in some way?

Not selling gave me so many possibilities.

I could use the company as a platform to raise awareness of different causes. Perhaps I could help start a movement to get people physically involved in various social or environmental projects, like building many more homes in Mexico for the homeless or helping the needy in our home city of Vancouver. I could use my platform to do more philanthropic work, maybe even connect with orphanages around the world and the indigenous peoples of the Amazon and North America to protect their ways of life. Most important, I could use my company to increase awareness of environmental and global warming issues, the need for policy changes and increased government involvement. I could use it to get people thinking in terms of the triple bottom line of people, planet and profits.

If I keep Aqua-Guard, I keep my credibility as a founder of a globally recognized company. I can open doors to meet with influential people all over the world. Those doors won't open the same way for me if I become a former business owner or a "consultant".

Over the years, we had risked it all, time and time again, for the survival of the business. Now I knew that I had to risk the business itself for what *really* matters.

My platform is priceless. I just cannot let it go to the highest bidder.

Aqua-Guard was not for sale.

But how to get out of a done deal?

Fortunately, there was a loophole. Vikoma had given us a non-refundable deposit to close by a certain date. That date had passed. I had called the owners in London and stated that they were long past the agreed closing date. My intention now would be to fly to London to meet them face-to-face.

When I arrived in Vikoma's London boardroom in February 2011, it was still early morning. A platter of bacon sandwiches greeted us for breakfast. As the owners tried to explain to me why they had not been able to close, I listened intently. Eventually, I stopped chewing. There was only one thing left to say and I said it. "I've had a change of mind and we're pulling the deal off the table."

It wasn't until the British Airways flight attendant once again asked me if I wanted "chicken or fish?" on my way from London's rainy Heathrow terminal 5 back to Vancouver that I turned my attention to what was next.

> *What am I going to tell LP? He wanted out. We had sold. The deal was done.*

I knew LP would have been happy with the cash because he was ready to move on. But I wasn't. I needed to fill my soul. During the flight home, I had to figure out how to make sure LP got what he wanted, while I kept the company as a platform for doing what I needed to do.

Back in Vancouver, I called LP and Cam into our upstairs boardroom and broke the news to them both as painlessly as possible.

"The deal is dead. I pulled it off the table."

LP's face went white. Silence. And then he spoke, "I can't accept that."

I was prepared for this.

"Are you still interested in selling your shares if I find a buyer?", I asked. An emphatic "yes" was his response.

"I'll come back to you with something soon," I promised him.

As the brief meeting broke up, I asked Cam if he and I could have a chat outside. The sun shone down on us as we headed up the street in front of our North Vancouver office building. Here was a guy who had come up through the ranks, who had helped pull us out of the fire in 2008 and got us back on track after the fraud. Here was the leader who had been running our operations for the past few years and who now knew all the ins and outs of our business better than I did.

From my perspective, Cam would be the perfect partner for the future, a young, eager and motivated self-starter who also had our team's respect. I asked him about the possibility of buying LP's 33% share of the business.

"Cam, I want you at the helm. And I want to slip back out of the day-to-day operations and only be involved in the things I enjoy and am really good at. If you can't manage the share purchase on your own, I'll help by buying back some shares, if necessary."

I paused to let my words sink in. "I think amazing things will happen if we re-structure the company this way...."

Cam, ever thoughtful, walked a few moments in silence before responding. "I appreciate you thinking of me. I agree that together we can build a great company. But I want you to spell out exactly what you want your duties with the company to be." So when we walked back to the office, I drafted a one-page plan of my future duties and gave it to Cam to review. He signed off on it and we shook hands.

Together, we called LP back into the boardroom. I opened with a few words: "LP, there's a potential buyer in the room with us." He looked at me and then he looked at Cam and got it. "If Cam can put a deal together to buy out your shares, I'll stay on as his business partner," I concluded.

LP smiled and the two of them fell into discussing details. Over the next few days, they agreed on a price. And within a month, the deal was complete. The closing happened on February 28th 2012.

Aqua-Guard now had a great, motivated young leader in the driver's seat of our "bus". We also had the right people in all the other seats. My agreement with Cam was that we would both receive dividends relative to our ownership stake and that we would pay ourselves salaries relative to how much sweat equity we put into the company on an annual basis. Since I would no longer be involved in the day-to-day, my salary would drop. You could say I bought my freedom that day.

I had failed at leadership succession in the past. Parachuting in GMs and CEOs from other companies hadn't worked. But this time was different. I had finally realized the best thing for the company and myself was to promote from within. Cam was the man for the job: he had been with us since fresh out of high school at 18. From the shop floor he had worked with all our suppliers and many clients in far off lands. He knew our costing and had the numbers smarts to do accurate estimates. Cam evolved from production and was learning the sales side of things. After fifteen years with us, he had developed into a very well-rounded businessman. The perfect guy to lead Aqua-Guard into the future. All I had to do now was take a step back and let him drive.

I found it difficult to let go during the first few months after this corporate restructuring. I had, after all, put my heart and soul into the business for almost 30 years. So my ego found it a bit tough to not be holding the center all the time. But gradually, over the next two quarters of 2012, I stopped coming in on Fridays so I could spend the day with Rieko. Then I scaled things back to two or three days a week.

They say Nature abhors a vacuum. Well, the blank space on my calendar didn't stay blank for long.

Even though I wasn't going into the office every day, I was soon as busy as ever. I got more involved with Homes of Hope, Covenant House and another local non-profit called Motivated by Wisdom/Teen Journey. Hockey, football and rugby with my sons took up more chunks of time. I decided to step up and play a bigger advisory role with the Pachamama Alliance by joining their Stewardship Council. And that led to meeting and getting involved with a Peruvian shaman named Jhaimy and his partner Starr in Vancouver, who run a foundation called "The Children of the Seven Rays" to connect communities in Peru and Canada and bring ancient and contemporary wisdom together.

And that wasn't all that was keeping me from the boredom of the golf course.

Bonny Meyer, the founder of Silver Oak wineries in California whom we had met on our Amazon journey in 2010, had told me about Hollyhock, a retreat center just up the coast from Vancouver on Cortez Island. Bonny visited us in Vancouver in the summer of 2012 and insisted that I meet Joel Solomon, the guy who ran the place, and his wife Dana. I found out later that Joel was very well connected politically in the province. I really respected Bonny: she is extremely wise and connected to something that I cannot explain. And she is certainly more evolved than I am in terms of understanding social connections.

I laughingly told her that I felt I was being pulled in two different directions. Earlier that week a group called Tiger 21, an affluent business group for high net worth individuals, had approached me and asked if I wanted to be a founding member of their new Vancouver chapter. They were also very politically connected, but more to the right wing side of things. The organization was strong in the U.S. and was now breaking into Canada.

Bonny was the one who put it all into perspective for me.

"Can't you see this is happening for a reason, Nigel?", she asked. "You need to join Tiger 21. And you need to go to Hollyhock. You have to listen to all points of view if you want to make educated decisions. And the only way to learn from the left and the right is to be immersed in both."

I balked at the idea. "Although I was raised in a somewhat right wing family, I really don't feel comfortable there. These days I am being pulled more to left of center." But Bonny was serious. And so I took her words to heart and became a founding member of the first of four Canadian Tiger 21 chapters.

Our chapter members included a mix of guys from many industries. We made up a very relevant group in terms of wealth and wealth preservation. Some had existing businesses they were still running: others had already sold theirs. Just like my Entrepreneur's Organization forum group, we all respected each other for who we were and what we had accomplished.

As always when I'm with new people, I initially felt quite uncomfortable. But I was soon enjoying the camaraderie and learning that come with being part of a community. Of course, as with most any group of people, there were differences among us, just as there were commonalities. My point of view was always just left of center, while most of the others were more to the right. On occasion, the guys would jab me about being the "greeny" of the group. I willingly accepted that role: we all were making a huge difference in the world in our own ways. The point of our gatherings, like those of the Entrepreneurs' Organization and the Gathering of Titans, was to put ourselves out there in uncomfortable conversations, to look at the tough issues, to force ourselves into dialogues where we actually could get the most learning and, eventually, understanding of other, sometimes opposing, opinions. Through it all, we became quite close.

It wasn't until I attended an annual Tiger 21 convention in Scottsdale, Arizona that fall with Rieko that the differences in our worldview really hit me. Participants from all over the U.S. and Canada came together every year as one big group for several days for a series of sessions. It seemed to me that the prevailing mood of the event was fear. The biggest concern for almost everyone was of losing what they had earned and built. Many who'd gone through liquidation events had since come to realize that the tax burden was bigger than they expected. With their business gone, they had no recurring income. All they had was a rapidly diminishing pile of cash. The issue was that this pile of cash, no matter how large it was, was not bringing in as much interest and dividend income as their operating business had. They perceived scarcity and so, like children in a sand box who've waited and worked hard to build the castle of their dreams, they were inclined to be very protective of what they had.

I have since seen many extremely wealthy people, mostly men, caught up in the paranoia that a scarcity mindset can generate. The feeling of terror underlying many of their conversations comes from a belief that what they have worked for will stop growing at the rate they have become accustomed to. That fear of the future, a future in which money will be scarce, just seems to lead to more hoarding, more protectionist behaviors.

This mindset of scarcity seems to be quite common with individuals who are highly successful in business. It is as if people who achieve great monetary wealth are more likely to become paranoid about all their hard work and earnings disappearing. I have seen wonderful, talented people build walls to protect their wealth, walls that isolate them and their families from the world. Why, with all their money and an obvious abundance of possessions, do they end up hoarding as if everything will be in scarce supply? For them, enough never seems to be enough.

Throughout my career, I have also witnessed a massive hoarding of wealth globally among the oil companies. The gap between the wealthy and the poor always seems to be widening drastically everywhere. The year before I joined Tiger 21, the first Occupy protest in New York City had caught worldwide attention. The 1% had suddenly come to mean the top 1% of the planet's population who have everything. Non-violent protests and occupations were happening in public spaces in countries all over the world in defiance of social inequality. The youth of the world were rallying around a declaration: "We are the 99%."

As Rieko and I left Scottsdale for San Francisco and our first Pachamama Alliance's annual fundraising event, we were very aware that we had become part of the 1% and that an undertone of civil unrest was brewing. In the midst of all this, I remembered something I had read in Lynne Twist's book *The Soul of Money*. She said that money comes and goes and it should "flow through you like water". Use money to do good and it will flow back to you just like it left. It wasn't until a few days later when we were in San Francisco that I fully understood what she meant.

The spirit of the crowd at the Pachamama fundraiser was overwhelmingly positive, a sharp contrast to what we had just experienced. Here were over 1,500 people gathered together, connected in their intention to do well by doing good. The joy of the group was palpable and powerful.

After the lunch, Rieko and I met several people, including fellow Vancouverite Shae Hadden (who later became my editor for this book) and Paul Herman. Bonny Meyer introduced me to Paul as the author of a recently published book about impact investing called *The HIP Investor: Make Bigger Profits by Building a Better World.*

Paul intrigued me and we got into a brief discussion right then about what impact investing was. HIP stands for "Human Impact + Profit". Basically, it's about choosing your investments based on future risk, return potential and the net impact on society. It's the last criteria that makes this kind of investing socially sustainable. He suggested that I look at what I was already invested in and, if I could, switch over from any "dirty" and socially unsustainable companies to clean and socially sustainable ones.

When I got back to Vancouver, I reviewed my investment fund portfolio based on the HIP criteria. Like many people, I was invested in mostly dirty industries and banks. This irked me. Here I was, the "environmental" guy, directly supporting companies involved with the Tar Sands, oil pipelines and fracking. I had to do my part to help the planet. So I called my broker and started moving my investments over to clean tech, organics and renewable energy.

That done, I realized something else was still bothering me.

Aqua-Guard was now running mostly without me. I had shifted away from the day-to-day ops and was hungrily feeding my soul by supporting my ideologies. I felt like a newborn activist. I had both feet firmly planted in my philanthropic endeavors. I felt passionate about so many things—from the environment and sustainability to homelessness and youth—that I found myself getting involved in almost everything that came across my path. I wanted to be involved in every endeavor I possibly could to save the planet and people—all at the same time. I couldn't seem to slow down. I had said "yes" to so many people that I found myself involved in more things than I could manage.

I had bought my freedom from Aqua-Guard. I had scaled back from an insane business life. Yet, in spite of my good intentions, I had evolved into a busy-ness that was proving to be just as crazy.

CHAPTER 13

A New Era

A few months after I stepped out of the day-to-day operation of Aqua-Guard, Daniel Koupermann called from Quito in Ecuador. He and John Perkins were going to be leading a trip to Tikal, the ruins at the center of the ancient Mayan world in current day Guatemala, for the changeover of the Mayan calendar at the winter solstice (December 21st 2012). They wanted to know if I'd be interested in going.

Some people believed this date marked the end of the world. Daniel and John, however, were inviting me and my family to Tikal to witness the end of a 26,000-year cycle and the beginning of the thirteenth baktun, the next "mini"-cycle of 144,000 days in the Mayan calendar. They, like the ancient Mayans, believed December 21st 2012 would be a turning point when the modern world of technology would start to learn to work together with age-old wisdom from indigenous communities around the globe.

Something about the vision I had that night in 2010 deep in the Amazon made me very curious to visit the ancient Mayan world. Since then, I had had recurring dreams in which, through swirling smoke, the smiling and then serious face of a Buddha would appear in the middle of the Mayan calendar. To be invited into the center of the Mayan world at this point in time seemed to be a bit more than a coincidence. I needed to explore this further. I asked Rieko and the kids if they wanted to go on yet another journey with Daniel.

They all jumped at the chance.

We touched down in Guatemala City on December 13th. Disembarking the plane, I did a double take. On the wall at the end of the tunnel leading off the plane was a large Mayan calendar—exactly as I had seen it in my vision, minus the smiling face of the Buddha.

I had no doubt I was supposed to be here.

We had arranged to stay in a charming inn in Antigua, a small enchanting mountain town just outside of Guatemala City, to get acclimatized. Our third-floor room, decorated with a small Christmas tree and some beautifully hand-painted ornaments, overlooked a narrow cobblestone street. From our veranda, we could smell sweet cooking aromas wafting up from a local street vendor below our window. Off to the left, a view of a large steaming volcano high above the town made this one of the most unconventional locations I had ever been in during the Christmas season. For the next few days, we explored the surrounding highlands and visited with local indigenous people in this UNESCO World Heritage site.

The morning of December 17th found us heading off to Tikal, 188 miles north of Guatemala City. We boarded a small plane in the city and flew for a short while through air thick with oxygen from the rainforest below. After landing in Flores, forty miles southwest of the ruins, we all created a chain gang with Dylan and Devon up front and the two of them tossed our gear up to Daniel, who was standing on the roof of our van. Daniel tied everything down with ropes for the drive to Tikal. Late that afternoon, we arrived at a small inn on the outskirts of the ancient city.

Before leaving Vancouver, I had done a bit of research on Tikal. It seemed to be an amazing, magical place, although now it appeared to be mostly hidden in thick jungle. Here the Mayans had ruled one of the largest empires in the world from about 2,000 B.C. to 900 A.D. If you look at the map today, their empire covered all of Guatemala and Belize, western portions of Honduras and El Salvador, as well as most of southeastern Mexico. The topography of the region included highlands (the Sierra Madre), lowlands (the Yucatan Peninsula) and the Pacific littoral plain.

Surprisingly, the Mayans established Tikal as a large urban center in a location where there were no waterways. For centuries, they relied on rain for their water supply, which was collected in large reservoirs and then transported via a system of aqueducts to various areas of the city. They had infinite patience and a deep respect for Nature and the heavens. They developed a calendar based on a 26,000-year cycle through meticulously observing the night sky and, seeing that it is not fixed, realizing that the earth moves one degree every 72 years in relation to its constellations.

So why would such a sophisticated people build a city that would be at the forefront of their civilization in such a strange spot? One theory suggests they believed Tikal was a massive center where cosmic energy was grounded to Mother Earth.

There are many theories about why the heart of Mayan civilization collapsed. The one that seemed most reasonable to me that first night in Tikal sounded ominously familiar. The Mayan empire grew rapidly in the century running up to 900 A.D. Experts believe that overpopulation and intensive agriculture led to environmental decline. Deforestation in the region around the city not only caused erosion and soil depletion. Cleared land absorbs less solar radiation, which in turn means less water evaporates to form clouds, which in turn makes rainfall scarcer. With no natural water source in the region, the civilization was doomed to fail.

During our first night in Tikal, Daniel wanted to take us into the old city so we could see it shrouded in darkness. We grabbed flashlights and disappeared deep into the jungle. Overhead, through the canopy of trees and vines, we could see billions of bright stars lighting up the Milky Way.

Eventually we came to a small clearing. In the darkness, we could make out the silhouette of a giant pyramid. Slowly, reverently, we approached it. Daniel, hunting for an opening, walked around the outer base. He pointed his flashlight at an inky blackness about six feet high and three feet wide. This was the opening, overgrown with vines and plants. It could have been a scene straight out of an Indiana Jones film.

Daniel invited us to turn off our flashlights and make our way, single file, down a long and narrow passageway through the pyramid to a small amphitheater on the inside. Without our lights, we had to trust our other senses. I heard each one of us take a deep breath before we entered the pitch-blackness. I placed my hands along the slimy walls and shuffled my feet along the slippery ground, moving deeper and deeper inside the pyramid. The deeper I went, the stronger the smell of the damp air became. I remember how grateful I was to get close to the end of the passageway and see the stars emerging from the inky black. As soon as I exited the long chamber, I immediately took in a deep breath of fresh jungle air.

As each of us emerged from the tunnel, we joined in a circle. And then we all stood quietly together for a few minutes before beginning the climb to the top of the pyramid. Once there, we lay on our backs gazing straight up through the crystal clear sky at the countless stars above. I could hardly believe what we were doing: lying on top of a Mayan pyramid witnessing one of the most stunning views I had ever seen. These were the same stars that the Mayans had viewed from the same spot thousands of years before us. And we were doing this only a few days away from the changeover of their 26,000-year calendar.

The next morning, we were excited to enter the ancient city and see the famous Jaguar Temple in daylight. We hiked through the jungle for about thirty minutes to a remote pyramid and then settled on the ground to listen to John tell us more about the upcoming changeover. He said that back home, in our modern world, many people were predicting Armageddon, the end of the world, in a few days. He explained that the Mayans had not predicted the end of the world: they had only noted that December 21st 2012 marked the end of one era and the beginning of another. And the next baktun would be a new renaissance during which the prophecy of the Eagle and the Condor would come into play. The Eagle (those following the path of industry, science and technology related to our modern world) and the Condor (those following the path of indigenous wisdom, intuition and introspection related to our natural world) would have to learn to fly together in the same sky. Exactly what the elders in the Amazon had told us three years before.

John asked us all to each find a spot in the jungle and sit for half an hour to think about the new era of the Eagle and the Condor and what our part would be as we move into the new baktun. I wandered in the jungle for a bit, not knowing where to sit down to think. I was feeling a bit off. I couldn't really get into what Daniel and John had been sharing with us about the mystical teachings or Mayan thinking. During the last 30 years of my business career, I had witnessed so much environmental degradation all over the planet. I was starting to think that maybe things are just too far gone and that the whole Eagle and Condor thing, the idea of the two worlds coming together to save the planet, was wishful thinking. My mind was racing.

> *We humans have been short-term thinkers for thousands of years, going back to the days when we first invented agriculture. Now it's clear to me the reason the Mayans disappeared was also short-term thinking: they cut down most of the trees in their ecosystem and changed their climate. The same perhaps for the inhabitants of Easter Island.*

Today we are doing the same thing—but on a much grander scale. We have complicated things not just by ravaging the planet, but also by polluting it for the sake of quick profits and shareholder satisfaction.

Things have to get really, really bad before we start to make changes. China is now leading the race in developing renewable energy sources like solar and wind. Why? Air pollution is so bad in Beijing that they have had to put up giant TV screens around the city to project images of the sunrise and sunset. Without these screens, people would never see the sun.

The energy sector is the same. Things have to get visibly bad before large corporations will invest in the long-term health of our planet and our collective future. Why do massive accidents like the Exxon Valdez spill in Alaska in 1989 and the BP Horizon accident in the Gulf of Mexico in 2010 have to happen before large oil companies will invest in upgrading their environmental response capabilities?

We desperately need to start changing our ways.

But we seem to be way past the tipping point. As Lynne Twist once mentioned to me, 1987 was the year when humanity started eating into the planet's 'capital' and using more resources than the earth can regenerate. I doubt that our human race can do anything now to slow down climate change: the issue is bigger than us. **Prevent** *climate change? This morning, climate change seems like too big a problem to even comprehend....*

I finally found a tree that looked comfortable to lean against and took a seat against its trunk. I closed my eyes for a minute and tried my hardest to think about what John had said. I took several deep long breaths to slow down and focus.

A year ago, I thought I finally had obtained my freedom. Yet here I was, acting like a "born again activist", full of conviction, running around trying to save the world with no real clear sense of direction. I had gotten involved in many causes. But what effect would all this activity really have on the world? Was the small part I was playing really going to change anything?

I took another deep breath and opened my eyes.

I looked down to see a stream of cutter ants passing by my feet, single file, on their way to somewhere.

> *How could I not have seen them when I sat down? How was it that I had not stepped on them?*

Each ant was carrying either a large piece of leaf or a stick. I had only been there a few minutes and they had already rerouted their path around my feet to continue on their way. I watched them for a moment, then took the steel bracelet I was wearing on my wrist and used it to block their path. I wanted to see what they would do. The lead ants stopped for a moment, confused. Then they sensed their way around the obstacle and kept moving forward, always on task, focused on bringing their load to the end goal, their nest. I was mesmerized by this amazing demonstration of Nature at work. Every ant had a strategic part to play in the chain. Each one had its own part to play in the collective. And yet, when one couldn't carry on, they figured out a way forward together.

> *What if we humans are like these cutter ants, each of us a piece of a larger collective, working together toward the same end goal? Those of us who are awake to the need for change are all doing our part—no matter how big or small. We may not all come into contact with each other as we help make changes in the world, but collectively we will make a massive difference to society and the long-term health of our planet. Our task is to have discussions with those still living in the illusion of the short-term world and work with them to see the importance of the long-term health of the planet.*

I looked down and lifted my bracelet from the path of the ants and placed it back on my wrist. Gently, I rose from my resting place, trying not to tread on their path as I headed back towards my group at the base of the pyramid. I was so moved by my insight that I couldn't share it with the group until much later.

Together, Dylan, Devon, Kina, Rieko, I and our new friends Saul and Dianne climbed to the top of the pyramid. We looked out over the expansive jungle and lingered there, silently watching the penultimate sunset of the Mayan baktun.

Tomorrow would be the most significant New Year's Eve in history.

We awoke on December 21st 2012 in our small bungalows to the smells of fresh Guatemalan coffee and the tropical rainforest. Over coffee, we shared stories of the previous day with our new friends and readied ourselves for the big day. A mini-bus was waiting to take us to Lake Petén, about a sixty-minute drive from Tikal.

When we arrived in the early afternoon, we still had a few hours to prepare before the evening ceremony. So Dylan, Devon, Kina and I grabbed a few kayaks and went for a nice paddle along the edge of this unique lake.

As evening approached, we returned to camp and began preparing ourselves for the last sunset of the 26,000-year cycle. All dressed in white, as instructed, we gathered at the edge of the lake and sat in quiet meditation. Our shaman came around and gave each of us a handcrafted clay bowl containing flower petals. He then led us as a group into the lake in our white attire. We walked out further into the cool water, the muddy bottom squelching between our toes, as the sun started to set on the mountains across the lake. From a distance, we must have looked like some cult entering the water. But all we were doing was giving thanks, cleansing the past and welcoming in the future baktun.

As the sun shone its last light on the previous 26,000 years, we slowly submerged ourselves in the lake, freeing all the flower petals to rise to the surface. We sat quietly in the water, watching the sun sink, surrounded by beautiful floating petals. We started to laugh and splash each other. I went for a long swim out into the middle of the lake with our kids as the rest of the group celebrated closer to shore.

The new era of the Eagle and the Condor had begun, and I was being drawn in the direction of the Condor.

The journey to Guatemala gave me yet a few more pieces to add to my understanding of purpose. I had just turned 50 before our trip and, after passing that landmark birthday, something in me started to feel compelled to share my life learnings with anyone who would listen and to share my platform of influence with whoever and whatever needed it most. In hindsight, these inner promptings were the first stirrings of my transition into the role of "elder", something we seldom recognize in our "Eagle" culture, but which is an integral part of the way of the Condor. This new adventure into "eldering" started to unfold with a phone call from Joel Solomon in June 2013.

Joel rang me, seemingly out of the blue, to ask if I would be a speaker at his Social Change Institute at Hollyhock. He wanted me to share my life story, basically a shortened version of this book, with his group. I somewhat reluctantly agreed and, a few weeks later, grabbed a floatplane out of Vancouver to make the 45-minute journey north to pristine Cortez Island, just off the coast of British Columbia. We landed on the ocean with a few bumps and beached the sixty-year-old Beaver. I quickly jumped down onto the pontoon and walked to the end of a float, took off my shoes and rolled up my pants, then jumped into the water to my knees and waded ashore with my duffle bag.

An older gentleman, a Hollyhock employee, was waiting just off the beach. He welcomed me and two other attendees who were getting off the floatplane. We all threw our bags into the back of his Prius and jumped in. As the old hybrid meandered down the single lane dirt track, I could smell the sea air. Our driver told us a bit of the history of the island and the non-profit educational institute we were headed for. Owned and run by Joel and his wife Dana, Hollyhock had been designed to bring social game changers from all over the world to this small island to share their views on politics and the environment.

When we arrived, I could tell that Hollyhock was run a bit like a high-end camp. There was a main meeting hall built in a style similar to an indigenous gathering hall, a lodge for eating and conversing, and several small residential cabins. In the back of the property, there was a large area for guests to camp, if they desired.

I felt a bit out of my element. I really didn't know anyone except for Joel, whom I had only met once for coffee. But after attending the evening sessions with the group of approximately 100 people who were on site, I started to feel a bit more at ease.

Although I had my own room and a very comfortable bed, I had a difficult time sleeping that night. I knew I would be the first speaker on deck in the morning. The focus would be on me for 90 minutes. I would present, a panel would quiz me, and then the floor would be opened to attendees to ask questions. I usually get nervous before I have to speak in front of a crowd, stemming from my childhood history with dyslexia. This time was no different.

The next morning, I was amazed that the attendees, many of whom were high-profile social activists, members of the BC legislative assembly and even a federal member of parliament, were all fully engaged in my talk. I got to the point in my life story where my company was pretty much running without me and I was now able to leverage it as a platform to do good. I was passionately involved in all sorts of global social causes. I told them that my volunteer and philanthropic work was catching up with me: I was exhausted playing the born-again activist. I wanted to support every cause that came across my bow and get involved in every board that wanted me, but before I knew it I was participating in more things than I could manage. I was busier than when I was in startup mode with Aqua-Guard. What had happened? Had I gained my freedom just to lose it again? Then I shared the insight from my experience with the cutter ants in Guatemala, along with the prophecy of the Eagle and the Condor, with them. I ended the talk with the realization that I had come full circle:

> "I'm doing more now than just living the entrepreneur's dream of financial freedom. I've always admired my good friend David Ash for his faith and philanthropic work. I've admired Bill Gates for stepping out of his day-to-day business at Microsoft to run the Bill and Melinda Gates Foundation. I've admired many other big-name world changers like Richard Branson with his taste for adventure, his humanitarian work and his Ocean's Unite initiative, Bill Clinton with his work transforming lives and communities, Leonardo DiCaprio for his environmental evangelism, Al Gore with his environmental activism, Robert F. Kennedy Jr. with his Waterkeeper Alliance and most of all Dr. David Suzuki for living his life's purpose in environmental activism. And, although I feel like small fry compared to these big names, I've been able to leverage what I've learned to help big picture causes in my own way. Together, we are all part of a collective of people making huge changes. And you too are doing your part to make the world just a bit better...leveraging your networks, companies and platforms to do good."

When my talk concluded, they pumped me with questions. The group's passion and genuine interest in me and what I had learned was overwhelming. I broke down in tears and hugged many of them. I really felt like I belonged here with this group of highly intelligent, fervent social activists. I was no longer alone: together we were part of the collective I had envisioned in Guatemala. Like the cutter ants, we activists are part of a massive human collective, each one of us doing our small part to create awareness and massive changes in the world.

I will never forget the last comment of the day. It came from Joel. He said he had seen many entrepreneurs follow a similar path and be "reborn" only to, eventually, burn out or give all their money away trying to help too many causes. He suggested to me (and everyone in the room), "Once people find out about you and the causes that you support, people will come after you for advice, for money, for time. They will want you to sit on their advisory boards. I know you want to make change happen right away. But this is not a race. So step back, breathe and take some time to be very selective about what you want to be involved with and how. Play the long game."

This suggestion to take care of myself and manage my new passions was some of the best wisdom I could have heard at the time.

Joel also got me thinking more seriously about how we might reverse the trends we humans have set in motion and invest in our collective future. I learned while I was at Hollyhock that he, like Paul Herman, managed a clean, socially responsible investment fund called Renewal that only invested in green tech, organics and socially responsible corporations certified as B Corps. After hanging out with both him and Paul, I really started to think about where to invest more of my portfolio. I still wanted to support things that made a difference and that generated a triple bottom line return (financial, social and environmental). Since I was looking to move away from dirty industries and into more sustainable ones, I became involved in Joel's Renewal funds after returning from Hollyhock.

With the blessings of Tiger 21, I invited Joel Solomon and his partner to give a presentation about social investing to my Vancouver Chapter. After that, I was able to invite Lynne Twist and Sara Vetter to speak about the "soul of money" to several of the other Canadian chapters. All these speaking opportunities opened up great discussions with everyone involved. Bonny had been right: I needed to be part of all these groups. I needed to listen and understand all the different points of view of each. Together, we need to create a mix of the best of socialism and capitalism so that the Eagle and the Condor can fly in the same sky and co-exist together.

CHAPTER 14
Freedom

Life was humming along in the latter half of 2013. Aqua-Guard was doing extremely well. Rieko and I were involved in many philanthropic endeavors around the world. Our kids were in high school and playing many sports. Everything seemed great.

But my EO buddies and I were still discussing one remaining concern we had: that our children would grow up with a sense of entitlement. We wanted to shake things up. We had taken our kids to Mexico more than a dozen times to help build homes for the homeless and volunteered with them to help David Ash and his family on the Vancouver's downtown East Side at Christmas. What else could we do to help shape them as "responsible global citizens"?

By the fall, I had been working with my coach Kevin Lawrence for almost ten years. I remember hearing Kevin's voice in one of our regular monthly calls innocently say, "Hey, you have one more goal that we have not talked about for a bit." I laughed and replied, "Oh yeah. What is that?"

"To take your family away for a year and travel the world." I laughed again and said, "Yeah, I forgot about that one!"

Kevin asked if I still wanted to do it. I paused to think before responding, "Yes, but I will have to check with Rieko."

Not one for delaying decisions, Kevin prompted, "Is she there?" I flipped back, "Yes, in the kitchen."

"So why don't you ask her?"

I put Kevin on speaker phone so he could hear her answer and then yelled, "Hey, Rieko! Kevin wants to know if you still want to take a year off and travel the world...".

She yelled back, "YES... of course!"

With that response, Kevin said, "OK. Let's make it happen."

"But, but, but, but...," I stammered. I came up with one excuse after another not to do it.

Kevin listened to them all and then offered, "We could work together on this and make it happen. The choice is yours."

I thought about what Joel Solomon had told me: take a step back, breathe and think deeply about your long game. Life is not a race. Taking a year to travel the world with my family would be the perfect "time out" to think and decide where my efforts would be most valuable moving forward. Also it would give me time and space to begin writing this book, something that people had been encouraging me to do for many years.

Rieko and I had made a decision back in 1994, just after our first son was born, that she would leave the business world and invest her time and energy in our children. That choice to become a stay-at-home mum was one of the most important decisions of our married life. Life with young kids is greatly rewarding, but it's not easy. Getting to a point where we could travel with them as young adults, spend close family time with them and explore the world for almost a year was the pinnacle of what Rieko had worked for. This wasn't just my dream: this was ours as parents. She and I agreed to treat this as another adventure, not making any specific plans beyond the first few steps.

Ever since I had taken Rieko to Tofino on Vancouver Island for a special 40th birthday celebration, our family had made it a habit of going there together for two weeks of summer surfing. So it came as no surprise to me when the whole family agreed that the Bennett world walkabout would start at the end of summer 2014 with a trip to this small west coast town for our annual surf pilgrimage.

Tofino's South Chesterman Beach is a very special place for us, but one night that summer made it extra special. Most days we liked to get a final surf session in here during sunset. By that time of day, most people had usually left the beach and we would have the surf break to ourselves.

This particular evening found Dylan, Devon and I sitting on our surf boards, snug up against the rock outcrop of South Chesterman, watching the silky swell push past the rock to create a perfect break. To my left, Rieko and Kina were boogie boarding a few hundred yards away. I began paddling effortlessly through the breaking waves on my 8'2" Pearson Arrow funboard, the cold northern Pacific water hitting my face and the fresh ocean smell invigorating my whole being. Glancing over to my other side, I could see Dylan and Devon breaking through each set of waves on their short boards right in sync with me. The three of us moved easily through the break and then sat up on our boards, ready to wait for the perfect swell to arrive.

There was not a breath of wind. In the quiet, we could hear Rieko and Kina laughing in the distance as they caught wave after wave on their boogie boards. Behind them, the sun was starting to set over Frank Island. The squeal of an eagle overhead spooked me. I looked up to watch it soar along in the ink blue sky. What an amazing place to be at sunset!

An offshore breeze began to pick up, pushing green waves up tall so we could see through them as if we were looking through glass. Over my shoulder, I caught a glimpse of a nice set heading our way. Dylan signaled to us that the next wave was his, and then he gently paddled and hopped up on the silky smooth surface. I nodded to Devon: the next wave would be his. With a few strong strokes, he was also up and away. Then the third wave in the set came for me. I started to paddle and then I was up, calmly riding my wave, green and clean, moving inexorably forever forward.

> *So much has changed in the past few years: I've gone from almost drowning in the Atlantic Ocean off Brazil's coast to calmly riding out this Pacific set with my sons. I've gone from almost drowning in my life and business to setting everything up so I could take this year off with my family without jeopardizing the company's future.*

I rode this perfect wave for quite some time. Finally, it broke and turned to white water. I did a kick and turned to drop back down on the board and paddle out again. I could hear Kina and Rieko yelling over at me, "Nice wave!" Silhouetted against the sun as it dropped into the ocean and turned the water orange, I could see Dylan and Devon both raising their hands to me in the surfer's salute. There was nothing between us and Japan but tangerine water and sky.

Cool waves hit my head as I paddled out once more to meet Dylan and Devon just past the break. We floated there, talking and laughing about our last ride, for a bit. A small porpoise came to play in the waves with us for a few minutes. He left as suddenly as he had joined us. Then offshore we could see the next set coming our way. This time the boys signaled for me to take the first one. I nodded back, smiling, and started to paddle with firm ease. With one final strong stroke, I was away and up, riding the face of my green wave against the backdrop of a now yellow-orange sky. The sun itself had completely disappeared from the picture, having dropped fully into the ocean. I kept ripping along, riding in all the way to the beach for a rest. With silent ease, I popped off my funboard and landed with both feet in the smooth Chesterman sand. I looked out past the break to see the silhouettes of Dylan and Devon as they thrust their arms in the air in approval. Glancing over towards the rock outcrop, I could see Kina and Rieko doing the same.

I picked up my board and walked backwards out of the surf, up the beach, all the while keeping my eyes glued to the four silhouettes of my family having fun. I could tell they were going to keep taking advantage of the silky smooth waves for a while. Except for a few families starting beach fires, we were the only ones enjoying South Chesterman.

Devon & Kina surfing - Tofino, Canada (2017)

I walked up the beach a bit to a log. The smell of softly burning cedar gently filled the air. I lay my board beside me in the sand, sat down and took a deep breath. Instantly, I was filled with emotion.

> *We've actually done it! I've been able to create the life I had dreamed of...thanks to the support of Rieko and my family, coach Kevin and so many others.*

Tears ran down my face into my mouth. I could taste the salt from my tears mixing with the residue of the ocean on my face. In only a few weeks, we would be off on a world journey very few get to experience. I was overwhelmed with gratitude.

It was spring 2015 and we were now almost seven months into our world journey.

We had been living for adventure off the beaten path. Surfing in Portugal, Indonesia and Brazil. Trekking in the Himalayas of Bhutan and the Andes of Argentina. Riding camels in Dubai, diving with scuba gear off a remote island in Indonesia, and jumping off a mountain in Argentina to paraglide. Kayaking in the rivers of France, Argentina and Colombia. We had sacrificed, de-feathered and made soup from a black Burmese chicken and eaten meal worms in Thailand. We had visited Rieko's tiny family village on the Sea of Japan and eaten freshly caught sashimi from the ocean. We had toured wineries and encountered many world cultures at restaurants in every country we visited. We had seen theater in London, art galleries in Paris, the Sistine chapel in Rome, and the Plaza de España in Seville.

The most difficult thing to leave behind had not been the business. It had not even been our dog Kaya, although that *was* tough. It was leaving behind the extended family we had formed over many years in our neighborhood. Our home had, over the years, become a second home to many of our children's friends and a "safe place" for youth in our community. Young people would visit, stay and even vacation with us. Our basement was a refuge for young people of all ethnicities—from Kina's girlfriends to Dylan's Wolf Pack and Devon's rag tag crew. Rieko and I (mostly Rieko) would listen without judgement to their daily stories and issues. She had become like a mother hen to many who arrived on our doorstep over the years. To this day, we have young adults in countries like Mexico and Venezuela who still call Rieko "Mumma". Leaving these youth for a year, although some did come and visit us along the way, was hard.

Kina (now 14 years old) and Devon (17) had both told us they wanted to attend acting school while we were on our world tour. Since Kina was being home schooled while we traveled, we set it up so they could do that for five weeks while we were in London. It was amazing to see them thrive as they spread their wings outside of the structured school system. Devon, who is also dyslexic and has ADD like me, came with me to every one of my business meetings. In some situations, I would find myself looking over at him and remembering my early exposure to the "real world of business" and the international trips my father had taken me on at about Devon's age.

During Devon's school years, he had missed more classes than he had attended due to anxiety, but on our world journey he completely opened up and flourished. He was a great person to have along with me. He got to wear a business suit when we sat down with international maritime organizations in London, coveralls and a hard hat in Brazil to climb the rope ladder from tender boats to offshore supply vessels where he would learn to operate our large offshore oil skimming systems. Allowing our children to make their own choices turned out to be one of the best decisions we made with them.

On the road, we were able to spend much time together. Pulling ourselves out of our "normal" daily routine gave Rieko and I the chance to sit for hours at a time in eclectic coffee shops, watching people and the world rush by. Time for us slowed to a crawl. At one point, we met another traveler who told us, "I am going to seize the day like a herd of turtles." Living in the moment allowed us to truly enjoy each other's company and our morning discussions just strengthened the bond between us. We met and befriended many locals along the way, people whom we easily fell into lively conversations with about travel, politics, and children and whose company we enjoyed.

On this particular morning, however, we weren't sitting in a coffee shop. I could tell from the white looks on their faces that Rieko and the kids were still pretty green from the bad roti they had eaten the night before deep in the Malaysian jungle. The large palm trees disappeared behind us as our flight lifted off from Kuala Lumpur International Airport (KLIA) en route for Yangon (Rangoon) in Myanmar. We had been deep in the Malaysian jungle for the past ten days and everyone in the Bennett family had been playing tag-team vomiting—except for me. As we left Malaysian airspace over the Adaman Sea on flight 740, I was the only healthy one in the family, but still my stomach took a turn. Just a few weeks prior, a similar Malaysian Airlines flight had gone missing somewhere over the South China Sea. It had not yet been found. This time we were flying into Myanmar, a country that had been known as Burma when it was under British control during the Second World War and which was now under the control of a military dictatorship. We were going to a country that had just recently been opened to outsiders for a few weeks of exploration. All it had taken was the suggestion of our new friends Peter and Roberto in London, England seven months earlier, to head us in this unexpected direction. They had given us the name of a local contact, a Mr. Han, who could help set up a visit for us.

Before leaving Vancouver, the thought of leaving Aqua-Guard and our home for a year had been beyond comprehension. Yet, once we were on the road, each of us with one small backpack and a single small suitcase that could be placed in the overhead bin of any aircraft, things became much simpler. Life actually became much easier. In most of the photos on our travel blog, you will see us wearing one of three t-shirts. We actually noticed that our clothes and shoes wore out over the year of travel.

The longer I was away from the Vancouver office, the longer the gaps between communications with them became. Heading into Myanmar, I knew these communications were going to be virtually non-existent for several weeks. But I was OK with it: my business had been running fine without me ever since we had left.

From my window, I could see the coast of Myanmar in the distance. As we approached land, I could see miles and miles of untouched rainforest with rivers meandering through the thick green covering. There was more visible evidence of basic industrialization as we neared Yangon. Touching down at the simple airport, we could see a high military presence alongside the runway. There were no gates, no boarding bridges. We deplaned down a mobile staircase onto the hot tarmac in the humid air of a land not many Westerners had seen. We were guided over to an old building, probably built before the Second World War, to claim our bags.

There, in the unconditioned air, we waited for our luggage and the used guitar that we had purchased in London to appear on the conveyor belt. I could feel the sweat rolling down my back while we patiently waited for that musical instrument, now famous for its ability to travel and arrive.

Eventually we had everything and were free to head for the customs and immigration counter, where we were greeted by a very cheerful agent who welcomed us to his country. Once through customs, we were released into a large hall packed with people waiting for family and friends arriving from Kuala Lumpur. We had arranged to meet Mr. Han here. We pushed our way through the crowd, looking for him. At first, he was nowhere to be seen.

> *Oh boy, my cell phone doesn't work here. We don't know where we are supposed to stay tonight. And I have no way of getting hold of this Mr. Han.*

Then suddenly a man wearing a long skirt (which we would later find out was a longyi, traditional garb for both men and women in Myanmar) was standing in front of us, a huge smile on his face. Mr. Han! He had his driver pick us up in a seven-seat minivan and off we went to our hotel. After checking in, we grabbed dinner locally so we could get to bed early. Our plan was to rise at 5 a.m. to fly from Yangon to Mandalay, the country's second largest city.

With Mr. Han as our guide, we spent the next few weeks touring all over this interesting country from north to south. Myanmar turned out to be one of the safest places we visited in our entire year-long journey. Driving through the dirt streets of Mandalay, we inhaled aromatic smells of food being prepared over open charcoal fires. The simple meals in Myanmar were outstanding, definitely the kind of cooking adventures that would get rave reviews from American chef Anthony Bourdain. The people were very straightforward and friendly, untainted as of yet by Western influences. Although they had lived for years under a brutal military dictatorship, there was a real innocence to them.

As part of our world walkabout, we wanted to get involved in some social projects in the countries we visited. We had been warned that Westerners need to be "very careful" when helping with social causes because in some places many of them are run and controlled by the local mafia. I had not yet run into this myself. When building homes in Mexico, we had taken an extra week to deliver food and supplies to a local orphanage south of Ensenada. And Paco and I, along with our local agents, had done the same for an orphanage outside of Rio de Janeiro in the past. But it made sense that organized crime would take advantage of the boom in "socially responsible vacations" and figure out a way to benefit off of do gooders.

We were lucky to have Mr. Han guiding us in who and what to give our money and energy to in Myanmar. We got to know his family, visited his village in northern Myanmar and knew that, when he recommended someone we could help, they were the "real thing". He suggested a Buddhist monk to us who had been single-handedly running an orphanage high in the mountains near his hometown for over 25 years. We went to a local grocery store and stocked up on food, supplies and treats for the children. When we arrived, Kina and Devon handed everything out. The feelings that got stirred up when we witnessed our children helping these orphans in such a pure, direct way can never be duplicated.

Kina & Devon at orphanage - Mayanmar (2015)

This day we were off to visit Bagan, the capital of the kingdom of Pagan from the ninth to the thirteenth centuries. Pagan was the first kingdom to unify the regions now known as Myanmar. During Bagan's heyday, over 10,000 Buddhist temples, monasteries and pagodas were built on its plains. Today there are over 2,200 temples and pagodas still standing, and the site could easily rival the largest religious monument in the world, Angkor Wat in Cambodia, as a tourist attraction.

We left our hotel rooms in the early morning mist at 4:30 a.m. Our van headed out into the plains along a dirt track that meandered between many stupas, mound-like structures containing religious relics. At one point, we stopped and everyone jumped out into the darkness. Mr. Han pointed at a large stupa with steep rock stairs carved into its side and said, "We are going up." Flashlights on, we began climbing hand over hand up the precarious steps until we reached a platform that gave us a view from high above Bagan. It was still quite dark, but we could make out the silhouettes of other stupas close by and then, as our eyes adjusted to the light, farther and farther out from where we were standing. There must have been thousands of stupas—big and small—scattered on the plains all around us. As the sun started to rise in the distance, we could see dots on the skyline. The sky was turning orange as the sun rose. Gradually, we could see the dots becoming larger and larger: they were hot air balloons carrying people across the plains. The combined image of these balloons and the stupas in the sunrise over the plains created one of the most amazing scenes we had ever witnessed.

We sat in quiet meditation for an hour, taking it all in, until the sun had fully risen to shine a warm hug on all our faces. Then we all looked at each other and smiled in silence. Mr. Han wordlessly gestured for us to climb back down. As soon as we hit the ground, the spell was broken and we were sharing our excitement about what we had just seen.

Mr. Han wanted to show us another special place. So we drove further down the dirt track between the stupas to a large arch. Here we stopped and hopped out of the van. A footpath led us to another large stupa with a massive arched entranceway. On the other side of the arches, we could see a large sitting Buddha inside yet another stupa. The expression on the statue's face was of this incredibly large, warm smile. As we approached the statue, that amazing smile was all we could focus on. As we got closer to the Buddha, the smile on its face changed to an expression of a very serious gaze. And then it hit me.

My 2010 vision from the Amazon (drawn by Devon)

This is what I had seen deep in the Amazon a few years before! This was the face of the Buddha I had seen in my vision. The face in the center of the Mayan calendar, the warm smile turning to a serious look projecting great responsibility over me. Suddenly, I couldn't breathe. I was having an anxiety attack. I had to stop walking and start consciously taking deep breaths.

I let the family and Mr. Han go inside while I sat for several minutes, staring up at the now serious-faced Buddha, trying to make sense of what I was seeing. When my family re-appeared, we all walked out together. But I walked backwards, looking back at the serious Buddha and watching as the expression returned to the warm smile we had seen from afar. The compassionate smile I had experienced at the Achuar village in the Amazon.

This was too far out there to be considered mere coincidence.

I can't explain everything that has happened in this spiritual ride through the universe that I call my life. And I definitely can't figure out what prompted me in the Amazon to envision a smiling, serious Buddha crafted by people thousands of years ago in a country I had never visited before. A country that had been closed to visitors for years.

I'm choosing to simply interpret the appearance of that tangible Bagan Buddha as a sign that I am on my correct path now. It has taken me a couple of decades, but I have finally come full circle, something I could have never imagined that day I broke away from my father's company back in 1992. I am now a father with my own children, young adults who I am proud to say have a set of values grounded in sustainability, stewardship and global citizenship, and who are starting to step out into the world on their own unique adventures without, I believe, a sense of entitlement or privilege.

I owe so much to the love of my life: Rieko. She and I have been a tight team since the day we met in 1988. We chose to make our life together a big adventure—and it has been. Through all the day-to-day struggles of living—of paying a mortgage, raising three children, starting a business and keeping it running—we have been able to continue stepping through those doors that deepen our relationship. And now our marriage is richly supported by all the relationships we have created together with people in our local community and in communities around the world. I am so fortunate to have found her. She is more than I could have hoped for as a wife, a mother, a friend and a life partner.

I have been awakened to the higher purpose and the greater responsibility we all share for our planet. With the support of many we have created an enterprise around protecting water, the world's most precious resource. With success comes an even greater sense of this responsibility: I cannot just sit back and do nothing with what I've created when I've been given so much and when there is still so much to be done. Keeping my business to leverage it as a platform for doing good I believe is the right choice. All the causes our family and friends support are in alignment with what we—together and as individuals—believe in and care about.

The world is changing at breakneck speed. Things that seemed daunting or almost impossible only a few years ago are becoming reality. We are inventing and bringing more and more sustainable, renewable energy sources and technologies online all the time—and these alternatives to fossil fuels are becoming more and more economical. The trickle down effect from just one innovation like solar roof shingles has the potential to significantly change our trajectory.

Even more important than the viability and significance of our innovations is the fact that awakened peoples of the world are pulling together. We now have 195 countries working to realize the terms of the Paris Climate Accord. At the United Nations' first conference dedicated to meeting the sustainable development goals on ocean health, nine of the world's largest fishing companies recently committed to protect the planet's oceans by pledging to prevent overfishing and help stamp out illegal activities. Google's "Project Sunroof" is now tracking who has solar panels on their roofs and how much they save in energy costs by doing so—and will soon be sharing that data with us. These are just a few examples of the nudges to be "good neighbors" and the new commitments to being fiscally, environmentally and socially responsible we are seeing in the news every day.

Our collective future depends on people awakening to the need to take care of our planet and each other to create a better world. People like you and me who dare to think the unthinkable and make changes—big and small. Who dare to keep making choices for the greater good of our children, our grandchildren and our great-grandchildren. For no matter who we are, no matter where or with whom we gather, no matter what we bring to this adventure called life, in our own unique way, one day we will depart knowing we did make a difference.

So why not just take that leap?

Gazing through a new lens

Sunset in Tofino

POSTSCRIPT

June 2017. As the chairlift ascends to the top of Whistler for my last back-country ski climb up Flute Peak this season, I look out over the thawing snow. A beautiful black bear, just risen from a long winter's nap, saunters over the exposed green grass. I know how he feels.

It's been two years to the day since our family returned home from circumnavigating this wondrous planet. And two years since I started making regular trips to Whistler to be alone in my "cave" for a few days at a time, serenely reflecting on what I've learned in life and trying to capture my thoughts in writing.

If you've read through this book from cover to cover, you are probably not a follower. You're probably a trailblazer. Now that you and I have climbed through the various pitches of my life together, it's time to unclip from the safety rope of a story, turn around and take a more expansive view of the key ideas we've covered together so you can blaze your own trail.

Over the past 35 years, I've been fortunate to have visited and conducted business in over 104 countries around the world. I have met people who truly live in dire poverty, without enough food to feed themselves or their families and without the support of other people or their natural environment. They exist at the edge of life, barely able to make enough to satisfy their needs. Success, for them, is surviving.

Deep in the Amazon rainforest, in Myanmar and in my home country of Canada, I have met other people whom I call "rich" but whom others call "poor". These "**rich poor**" lack access to cash, yet they satisfy their basic needs, care for their loved ones, steward their environment. They value more than just profits. Success for them is living in happy abundance, richly rooted in their family and friendships, their society and the natural world.

I have also met people in many nations around the world who have an abundance of financial resources, but who are trapped like gerbils in a never-ending stress wheel, trying to care for their loved ones financially and constantly striving to "arrive" at a place where they will feel safe in their abundance. A place which, they don't yet realize, does not exist. I call these people the "**poor rich**". Success, for them, is a constantly moving target.

If you are "poor rich", you were probably led to believe, like I was when I was growing up, that we can be whoever we want to be and we will be able to make as much money as we want. We are told, "The sky's the limit!" Our parents push us to graduate from high school with honors so we can get into the top college or universities where we are launched into the "real" world with grand expectations of fame and fortune, of having way more than simply what we need to survive. We are programmed to believe all we have to do is work hard, chase the almighty dollar, hoard and guard our earnings. Everything revolves around increasing our social status, impressing our peers and making our parents proud. This "poor rich" belief system is based on climbing up the social ladder as high as possible and accumulating as many possessions as possible in one short lifetime. That is success. Once we have it all, then, "they" tell us, we will find true happiness! They don't tell us that, living like this, we sacrifice the most important things in life, such as our health, family, community or, sometimes, even our ethics.

This programming gets us a living—but not a great life. And certainly not freedom. We can stick with this programming or we can, once we're aware that there are alternatives, choose something different.

For many years, I was stuck in this "poor rich" mindset of scarcity, always fighting to make ends meet and then, once they were met, to get to the next shiny object. In my mind, I was having a hard time living in the moment and being happy with what I had in the now. That is, until I realized what really mattered to me.

Many years ago, my coach Kevin asked me a really powerful question. "Nigel, if someone came and offered you $1 for your business right now, would you sell it to them?" My immediate answer was "Yes!" In that moment, I would have done anything for "freedom". I would have given everything up for the "freedom" to live the way I wanted to live.

For me, freedom is being able to do what you love and loving what you do. Freedom is having flexibility with your time. Freedom is the ability to be involved with the people and the causes you care about.

Since that coaching conversation with Kevin, I've broken free of my preprogrammed norms. Since then, I've been choosing freedom.

That didn't mean I had to quit my day job or close up my company. It meant I had to wake up to the most important things in life, to having the most positive impact in the world I possibly can, to creating a meaningful life for myself and my family. It meant I had to wake up to living my personal "why" and not wavering in that.

I'm not here to tell you what to do. I'm here to share. Every one of us was born into a unique set of circumstances. Every one of us has their own path in life. The choices I have made, although extremely difficult at times, have worked for me in mine: some or all of them may also work for you in yours. But I am not the one to make that call. You are. So here's a short summary of what I've learned and shared with you in this book. Feel free to take from my stories and this list what resonates with you and apply it to creating your own life.

1. **I chose to follow my own path.** I pursued my own dream and discovered my own life's purpose, my own big "Why?" or, as the Buddhists say, my dharma. I learned to break away from toxic and negative relationships. I now surround myself with helpful, positive and supportive people who nourish me. I don't waste my time in low-energy environments. I have worked hard to create something amazing, something with great meaning that fills me and those close to me with joy.
2. **I've created my own version of freedom and made it real.** I learned not to build my life around someone else's idea of what freedom looks like. For me, that meant building and setting up my career and business as a platform to do good so that I can selflessly serve others while having extraordinary experiences with my family. Ultimately, my intention is to leave the world a little better than when I arrived.
3. **I now view my life as a bold adventure.** I've surfed through an unpredictable world, sensed my way through uncharted waters, climbed my way towards unfamiliar achievements. This, for me, is the most exhilarating part of life. No matter how incredibly difficult the going gets, I've learned to be patient, to persevere and appreciate everything and everyone in the moment as a valuable part of my very own adventure.
4. **I've learned to push past my personal limits.** I've taught myself not to settle for comfort. I've chosen to be my authentic, unprotected self and to be constantly improving and "changing for the better" (what

the Japanese call "kaizen"). Every time we push ourselves to ride the edge of discomfort, our brains actually rewire. We evolve ourselves to be stronger, better prepared for the next time we encounter a challenge.

5. **It's been important for me to keep taking the next step.** I keep consciously inventing my way forward, one step at a time. At times, I sure have struggled to survive. But I didn't give up when luck wasn't with me. Just like in several of my life-and-death situations, magic happens when I put aside the urge to "freeze, fight or flee". When I hyper-focus and stay present, when I persist and get done what needs doing. When I let doors open in front of me, instead of forcing them.

6. **I ask for help when I get stuck.** I don't push people away. Coaches, peers and family keep me on my toes, inject me with new energy and ideas, and help push me into that sweet spot where I am in the zone of accelerated growth and learning. The place where the Universe's intentions for us just start to unfold naturally and easily. And when people ask me for help in the form of advice, I've learned to share and not tell people what to do. I give them the benefit of my experiences and my learning: I don't tell them what they "should" do.

7. **Now I fill my soul with love, joy, extended family and good friends.** I don't tie my self-worth to my business or money. Quick fixes of happiness or satisfaction are a poor substitute for what endures. I will never regret choosing love, joy, family and friends over work commitments.

I have discovered that it is possible to set up a business or a career that can become a conduit for doing good and amazing things in the world. It is possible to make a positive difference that will matter for generations to come. It is possible to be free. With a lot of self work, these have all been possible.

The only thing I would say to you is don't wait. Take that leap. Go and create a life of adventure and deep meaning. Make it incredible.

JUST REMEMBER ONE THING.

With great freedom comes great responsibility.

ACKNOWLEDGEMENTS

I owe everything great in my life to the network of support I have had around me over the years. Without all these people, I'd probably be divorced and broke by now. Without them, I certainly wouldn't have been able to set up my business and life so that I could do what I wanted with it.

Thanks to my family—nuclear and extended.

My parents Anne and John for taking a big risk back in 1966 and leaving the comfort of their Welsh homeland with three small children for the new land of Canada, a country which I am proud to say has been our home for over 50 years.

To my wonderful wife of almost 30 years, Rieko, for joining me in taking the biggest leap of our lives and saying "yes" when I proposed to her on Kokanee Glacier all those years ago during a heli-skiing trip in British Columbia's backcountry.

My kids Dylan, Devon and Kina for putting up with me in the early years while I was traveling all over the world for business and for growing up to become my best friends.

My sister Sue for being a good listener and my reality check, and for bringing her husband Garry into the Bennett clan.

My grandma Doreen for teaching me to always laugh and have a good time—no matter what the situation.

My Aunt Cherry and her family for supporting me throughout my life—and all the Bennett clan back in the United Kingdom with whom we still keep in touch.

The entire extended family of kids and their parents around the world who have come to trust Rieko and I—starting with our children's close buddies (like Kina's girlfriends such as Mackenzie Sheradon and others like Dylan's Wolf Pack and Devon's rag tag crew) and expanding outwards from there. A special shout out to Adan in Chicago for being a great inspiration for *all* our kids.

Thanks to my coaches—past and present.

Terry Jackson, my first business coach, for making a significant difference in my early career and for recognizing and graciously acknowledging when it was time for me to work with someone else.

Kevin Lawrence, my second executive coach and author of *Your Oxygen Mask First: 17 Habits to Help High Achievers Survive & Thrive in Leadership & Life*, for helping me clear up the minefield that was my life, work through my father issues, grow my business and, eventually, set it up to virtually run without me. Most importantly, for helping me stay focused on what was most important, make time for my family and achieve all my life goals.

Shae Hadden, my writing coach and editor and author of *The Blue Pearl: Getting the Most Out of Coaching*, for making this book happen and for being my friend.

Mike Michalowicz for his support and book promotion skills (author of *Profit First: Transform Your Cash-Eating Monster to a Money-Making Machine*).

Thanks to my business team—near and far.

All the staff at Aqua-Guard for always going the extra mile to make a difference.

Cameron Janz for being a good friend and for staying the course, rising through the ranks at Aqua-Guard and taking over the running of the business as my partner.

Co-founder and former business partner LP, for having the courage all those years ago to break away with me and Sue and for bringing his invaluable creative talent and technical skills to the table.

Larry Pintler and Joe Smith at NRC for becoming good clients, great friends and unshakable Aqua-Guard cheerleaders.

Thanks to my peers—the titans I've met along the way who became my life-long friends.

Many members of the Entrepreneurs' Organization and their families (known in the early years as the "Young" Entrepreneur's Organization), for opening my eyes to see that I was not alone. Special mentions go to Trevor Bowles for encouraging me to leap into belonging to YEO, Lance Bracken for inviting me into his No Limits Forum group and for always being a gracious host, and to my good friend David Ash (author of *Goodness Is Contagious: From Profit to Purpose*).

My classmates at MIT's Gathering of Titans (GOT) in Boston, founder Verne Harnish (author, *Mastering the Rockefeller Habits*), co-chairmen Mike Maddock (author, *Free the Idea Monkey*) and Rick Sapio, and Chuck Hall for keeping GOT fresh and on the edge.

All the members of Tiger 21 for holding me accountable for becoming the business leader and human being I wanted to be in the world.

Thanks to the fearless souls who have dedicated their lives to awakening the dreamer in all of us.

Lynne and Bill Twist, John Perkins, Daniel Koupermann, Sara Vetter and everyone at the Pachamama Alliance for taking a stand for the planet and for life itself and committing to creating a socially just, environmentally sustainable world.

My PachaLibre tribe for witnessing and supporting my awakening (you know who you are...Gloria, Trea, Lauren, Bonny, Sara, Brett, Ben, Dianne and Saul).

The Achuar tribe for helping us all understand how important it is that the Eagle and the Condor co-exist in these times and that we protect the way of life of our indigenous brothers and sisters and steward the land.

Thanks go to the tireless souls who have invited me into their circles to help them do good work in the world.

Sean Lambert at Homes of Hope for creating the possibility for me and my family—and for our many friends and their families—to give our time and energy to building homes for impoverished people.

Jhaimy and Starr at Children of the 7 Rays Foundation for giving me more opportunities to learn about and honor the sacred wisdom teachings of the Andes. (www.childrenofthe7rays.com)

Joel Solomon (author of *The Clean Money Revolution*) and the whole team at Hollyhock for making me feel comfortable in their environment.

And last, but not least, thanks go to the entire network of friends who have helped me, sometimes in zany and sometimes in profound ways, enjoy this adventure called life.

Jim Haberl for being a great inspiration to both myself and my sister.

Lynne and Donnamae Wilson for coaching me and my buddy Steve Marette to become the two youngest sailors in Canada to get our Gold Sail and to both become sailing instructors, as well for encouraging us to work as "mountain people" at Lake Louise way back in the late 1970s and early '80s.

Ken Legg for dragging me into so many dodgy places—and bringing me out alive.

Rob Jones, Ken Walton and Keith Walton for always pushing our physical and mental limits with great comedic flair.

My old Eagle Harbour gang from elementary and high school for accepting me for who I was without question and for opening up that acceptance to include my wife and children as your friends.

Dave McDonald, to whom I owe a great deal for introducing me to my life partner Rieko.

John Stiver, a one-in-a-million find, for patiently introducing our family to the power of music.

And the many more (you know who you are) whom I and my family love so much.

THANK YOU, EVERYONE.

ABOUT THE AUTHOR

NIGEL J. BENNETT is a multiple award-winning entrepreneur and a co-founder and principal owner of Aqua-Guard Spill Response Inc., a world leader in the design, fabrication and supply of state-of-the-art marine oil spill response equipment and services. Nigel boldly lives his personal "Why?" by being an advocate for environmental and social responsibility among the entrepreneurial tribes to which he belongs. While his company (aquaguard.com) protects the world's most precious resource, he speaks and consults with young people worldwide about bringing their talents to solving some of our planet's most pressing challenges.

An avid outdoorsman and adventurer, Nigel lives in Vancouver, Canada with his wife, Rieko, and their daughter and two sons.

Follow his ongoing adventures in business and in life by visiting **NigelJBennett.com.**

CPSIA information can be obtained
at www.ICGtesting.com
Printed in the USA
BVHW01s1721070218
507513BV00031B/1439/P